What Do You Think Would Happen...

Tim Beitzel

TRILOGY

Trilogy Christian Publishers

A Wholly Owned Subsidiary of Trinity Broadcasting Network

2442 Michelle Drive

Tustin, CA 92780

For information about special discounts for bulk purchases, please contact Trilogy Christian Publishing.

10 9 8 7 6 5 4 3 2 1

Library of Congress Cataloging-in-Publication Data is available.

ISBN 979-8-89333-098-4

ISBN (ebook) 979-8-89333-099-1

DEDICATION

To my wife, Melody, who has always been my biggest supporter, most honest critic, and truest partner in life and ministry.

TABLE OF CONTENTS

INTRODUCTION

I love the church. I grew up in the church. My mother taught Sunday School, sang in the choir, played piano, and led the youth choir. Her father, my grandfather, was a pastor in the church I grew up in, shortly before I was born. My parents met in that same church. It's really a funny story. My dad's younger brother visited the church one Sunday soon after my grandfather became the pastor. In a later conversation, my uncle told my dad about his visit and further informed him that the new pastor's daughter was very pretty. My father showed up shortly thereafter to validate his little brother's claim, and the rest became my history!

In short order, we all became an integral part of that church, Shepherdstown Evangelical United Brethren, located in Mechanicsburg, Pennsylvania. Dad, a carpenter by trade, could be found building or repairing something on the church property regularly. We went to every church function. I served in various capacities, was part of the youth fellowship, and first sang in front of people in church when I was about seven or eight years old. When I was 19, I formed a quartet with three friends, and we called ourselves "The Believers." Predictably, Mom was our pianist.

Church was a focal point for our family. On Sunday mornings, Sunday School was as well-attended as the worship service in which there was rarely an open pew. Vacation Bible School, evangelistic services, and special celebrations were common, exciting, anticipated, and well attended. I had the privilege of growing up in an era when it seemed like most people went to church. Until I grew older, I thought everyone grew up just like I did! Even so, with all of that going for me, it wasn't until I was 18 years old that I surrendered my life to Jesus. He then began a life-long process—which I hope is far from over—including a call to ministry filled with triumphs and disappointments, successes and failures, endings and new beginnings, and heartaches and blessings.

My testimony is a bit different than some. I knew I was called into ministry before I was saved. My exposure to genuine Christianity formed in me an unshakable belief in God and the need to be saved through the work of the cross, but I resisted making the decision to completely follow Jesus through my teen years, doing some stupid and careless things, about which you will have to forego reading. It was during my first extended stay away from home that I came face to face with the reality that not only was God calling me to a lifetime of ministry, but more importantly, I wasn't ready! It was in my bunk in a dorm room in Western Pennsylvania where I gave my heart to Jesus. I'd like to be able to say that I've never made any mistakes since then, but I would be lying if I did. There is no doubt, however, that a cold night in February of 1982 was the beginning of a brand-new life for me. Less than two years later, I began a 27-year journey of itinerant music ministry traveling throughout the US, Canada, Mexico and the Caribbean.

God called me off the road in 2010 to prepare for something I used to boldly say I'd never do—be a pastor. Having been to thousands of churches in what I jokingly referred to as "hit and split ministry," God had changed my heart and redirected my passion from visiting many churches to leading only one. One thing hasn't changed, though: my love for the church! I've always been called to the church, first as a musical revivalist, then as a pastor. I've seen churches rise and fall. I've made many pastor friends and have been crushed as some of them fell away from the Lord. God has seen fit to use me to exhort and challenge many people of all walks of life, some of whom I only met once, and God has blessed me to pastor the local church, where I get to invest in one group of people day in and day out.

I love the Church. That is the main reason for writing this book. I don't know if I'll ever write another. Sometimes, it seems like I'll never finish this one—but the Holy Spirit has prompted me to share some observations with you, observations about the past and current condition of the Church, and optimistic, high hopes for her future! It never ceases to amaze me that the holy institution which God ordained and Jesus established would be entrusted to fallible human hands, but that's just the point, isn't it? God created mankind with free will; He wanted a genuine relationship with His prized creation, not one that was one-sided. In the same way, the Church, imperfect though she may be, has to be administered by mere flesh and blood, lest the element of free will be removed.

There have been many great moves of God throughout history. There have been revivals, reformations, and awakenings, varied and diverse, but an unfortunate commonality pervades them all; they all end! We need to be continually renewed, continually revived, and that cycle will need to be repeated until Christ comes for His bride. I do believe, however, that we can learn some lessons from mistakes of the past. We *should* be able to do better. We, indeed, *should* be able to dream of and aspire to the *greater works* that Jesus said we would do in His name! Hence, the title of this work, humbly submitted, *What Do You Think Would Happen…* It is my earnest hope and prayer, that you will be encouraged to live each day with determination and expectation for what very well could be…*if.*

PART A:
WHAT DO YOU THINK WOULD HAPPEN...

CHAPTER ONE

...if The Church Walked the Talk?

Growing up in church, and subsequently spending over a quarter century "on the road" as an itinerant, in addition to pastoral ministry, I've probably heard every churchy expression there is. I'm sure you know what I mean; those spiritually appropriate declarations and responses to other people's spiritually appropriate declarations that can be heard regularly on any given Sunday inside the building we have come to call "the church." There's nothing inherently wrong with most of them (although some are downright unbiblical, like "God helps those who help themselves," and "God won't give you more than you can handle," but I won't get into that here). Church lingo varies greatly depending on tradition, culture, denomination, geographic location, language, and especially, age group. What is a common expression in America may mean little in Europe; what was widely understood in 1955 may not carry the same meaning today.

Regardless of these influencing factors, there's a commonality I've observed among people who show up in the church building on Sunday morning: *many of them don't believe what they're saying!* That's a strong statement, but it's one that I stand by, even if I must reluctantly include myself as one who has been guilty. It's probably not entirely our fault, as most of us who cut our teeth on the backs of pews have been slowly but consistently indoctrinated with the lexicon of acceptable church phrases to use when we hang out with other Christians of our brand. We learned most of these when we were children, perhaps not really thinking about what we were saying. Now that we're all grown up, however, it's time we either own what comes out of our mouths or simply remain silent.

Let's examine some frequently uttered church expressions and ask, "What do you think would happen, if church people actually believed what they said?"

"God Is Able"

This is most certainly a true statement. Often, we quote the scripture from Ephesians 3.

> *"Now to Him who is able to do exceedingly abundantly above all that we ask or think, according to the power that works in us, to Him be glory in the church by Christ Jesus to all generations, forever and ever. Amen."*
>
> *(Ephesians 3:20-2 KJV)*

When we declare "God is able," it asserts our faith and trust in an almighty God who created everything and who can alter even His own principles of physics and matter for the sake of His beloved children. This is a marvelous affirmation of the omnipotence of God, but we do well to digest the entirety of what this much-recited passage of scripture reveals. Not *only* is God Himself able, but He is *also* able to enable *us* to do what seems to be impossible, not because we ourselves are able, but because the Holy Spirit works *through* those who have been redeemed by Jesus Christ.

I'm afraid the walk doesn't often match the talk when it comes to the expression, "God is able." Most often it is declared as a last-ditch glimmer of hope when all else has failed, rather than a go-to first response to what appears to be impossible. If we are truly to believe and announce the eternal truth that "God is able" in the context of Ephesians 3:20-21, it needs to be walked-out in such a way that declares "I believe that not only can God *Himself* do anything, but also that He can accomplish it in and through *me* as I yield to His enabling Holy Spirit."

What does this look like? It's placing one foot in front of the other, anticipating the miraculous, and not making excuses for the ordinary. It's a heart attitude of confidence and expectation in the God of the universe to do what He's already declared, in His Word, that He would do. It's living out the confidence that God is at work, even when we can't see it with our natural eyes, even when we don't know how or when He's going to accomplish it. It's cooperating with Him by being obedient to His leading, even when His leading doesn't make sense. This doesn't happen by an act of our will, but by continuing to develop an active, growing relationship with a living God; it happens by allowing the Holy Spirit to grow us up and equip us according to His purpose and plan. What do you think would happen...if church people truly believed...that God is able?

"I'll Be Praying for You"

"Therefore, confess your sins to one another and pray for one another, that you may be healed. The prayer of a righteous person has great power as it is working."

(James 5:16 ESV)

I remember seeing a cartoon that depicted a pastor standing in the sanctuary of a church building chatting with parishioners when all at once, he noticed a man coming through the doors. The "thought bubble" above the minister's head read, "Oh no! That's John! I told him I'd be praying for him, and I forgot all about it! *Dear Lord, please be with John*!" and immediately, he greeted John with, "Hi John, I've been praying for you!"

If you're at all like me, you can relate. This must be fairly common and, in most cases, unintended. We get busy and we forget what we promised and hopefully, once we realize our error, we take the time to fulfill our pledge. I do wonder though, how many times the commitment, "I'll be praying for you," goes unfulfilled. Nowhere is this more pronounced today than on social media. A pair of folded hands shows up on the screen (or is that a high-five?), and heaven is instantly bombarded with petitions and supplications on behalf of our oppressed friends and loved ones. Probably not. What do you think would happen if every promised prayer made its way to the Throne Room of God? Wouldn't it be great if the phrase "I'll be praying for you" was taken seriously, as if it was vitally important and deemed necessary to the resolution of the issue at hand? God intends for prayer to be as natural as conversation with a friend. Why is intercessory prayer so often reduced to a catch phrase that sounds spiritual, but carries little promise?

"I'm Hungry for the Word" often accompanied by **"I'm Just Not Being Fed"**

Don't say these sentences. Ever. If you have, and/or do, stop. Immediately. Repent and ask forgiveness. The only excuse for being hungry for the Word of God is laziness. Even farm animals know they have to go to the trough to eat. If you're truly hungry for the Word, you will never utter the phrase; you will simply go to where the food is. If you're "not being fed," perhaps it's time to grow up and learn to feed yourself. What do you think would happen if people who say they are hungry for God actually were? I just don't see the need for further commentary on this one.

"I Want the Church to Grow"

"All the believers devoted themselves to the apostles' teaching, and to fellowship, and to sharing in meals (including the Lord's Supper), and to prayer… all the while praising God and enjoying the goodwill of all the people. And each day the Lord added to their fellowship those who were being saved."

(Acts 2:42,47 NLT)

There can be no question whether it is God's will for each local church congregation to grow. It is. All living organisms, whether physical or spiritual, *must* continue to grow. If they do not, they will die. There are, however, two ways to look at this subject of church growth, and that is because there are two definitions of "church." Stay with me.

If you've spent even a little bit of time in church, no doubt you have read or at least heard these words of Jesus spoken to the apostle Peter: "...upon this rock I will build my church and the gates of hell will not prevail against it." (Matthew 16:18 ESV) Jesus was speaking of the true Church comprised of all those who would truly believe upon Him as Savior and follow Him, transformed, indwelled, and empowered by the Holy Spirit.

The word that's translated *Lord* in Acts 2:47, *And each day the Lord added to their fellowship those who were being saved,* is from the Greek word *kyrios*, meaning, in this case, God. So, the first definition of *Church*, and the only one that the Bible speaks of, is that which was instituted by Jesus Christ, is being fueled by the Holy Spirit, and continues to grow by the hand of God. This Biblical true Church will never cease to exist. (*The gates of hell will not prevail against it.)*

There's another definition of church which you can likely surmise. It's the organized institution with the sign over the door; it's the one that hires staff, has Facebook, Twitter, and Instagram accounts, and is recognized by the government as a non-profit charitable organization. They are everywhere. Some have steeples, pews, organs, and sing hymns from a book; others meet in repurposed warehouses or converted movie theaters with stage lights, fog machines, and cutting-edge worship bands.

Whatever your tradition, preference, and experience, whether your pastor wears a robe or skinny jeans, no matter if you sing the songs of Charles Wesley or Chris Tomlin, this organization is the one most people are talking about when they talk about *church*...and talk about church they do!

True, there are some church people who see growth as a threat and do everything to avoid it. They soon get their wish as they watch their church dwindle and close, generally clueless of the reason why, but, by and large, most churchgoers freely state, "I want the church to grow."

So, which *church* are they referring to, and how much is it worth? What if it requires more money? *Their* money. What if it requires more effort? *Their* effort. What if it requires a change in priorities, methodology, nomenclature, style, building, or geographic location? I'm just getting started…what about working with other local churches in a way that people come to Christ and no one particular church gets the credit? What about an outreach to the community that doesn't result in an increase in Sunday morning attendance for *your* church? What would the supposed church-growth advocate do if *their* local church parented or planted another church, and *that* church outgrew the mother church? Would that bring a sense of success or failure?

There may be exceptions, but I have found that when a local church hasn't grown for a period of time, and the members quickly tell you that they want the church to grow, they don't mean it. What they really mean is, "We don't want to change anything about how we 'do church,' but we want different results." Those results have little to do with the Biblical definition of *Church*, the one that Jesus instituted, that the Holy Spirit empowers and that grows by the hand of God. The results they desire have more to do with their little corner of the market. Just consider, for a moment, all the Kingdom resources (that's a religious way to say money) wasted on man's kingdoms cleverly disguised as "church;" think of how that could be invested to *really* grow the Church… the one that Jesus is the head of.

Church buildings serve a legitimate need; denominations have their place; paid staff and church programs all have their role to play. I have met people who rail against some or *all* of these organizational building blocks to the degree that they base their righteousness on the fact that they *don't* participate in the man-made institutional church. When any group adds requirements to salvation beyond Christ and claims exclusivity within Christendom, that's a cult! But, when the focus isn't on Jesus and the lost people who need Him, can we genuinely refer to an organization as *The Church?* William Temple, Archbishop of Canterbury from 1942 to 1944, is famous for defining the "Church" as the only organization that exists for the benefit of its non-members.[11]

"I want the church to grow." What a strange statement when you think of it! If you told people you wanted your vegetable garden to grow, they would give you a blank stare. I mean, why *wouldn't* you want it to grow? Things that live, grow. If they don't, they die. So. What do you think would happen…if everyone who states "I want the church to grow" actually walked the talk? What if they availed themselves of the nourishment that would ensure growth? What if everyone who claimed to follow Jesus actually did so? What does it mean to follow Jesus? Why don't we see what Jesus Himself had to say;

> *"Then Jesus said to his disciples, 'Whoever wants to be my disciple must deny themselves and take up their cross and follow me.'"*
>
> *(Matthew 16:24 NIV)*

While we're on the subject of "talk," can we agree to resist the urge to make some declarations that can actually cause us *not* to walk in the right paths?

"Nobody's Perfect"

No kidding. That's why we need Jesus, but the attitude that initiates such a statement may just be denial of one's own unrepented sin; you know, a way to create an "out" for dealing with disobedience to God. It's true. Nobody *is* perfect, except Jesus, and that's *exactly* why He was made propitiation for our sin, but a living relationship with God through Jesus Christ does not stagnate; it continues to transform us so that we continue to look more like Jesus every day.

"But we all, with unveiled face, beholding as in a mirror the glory of the Lord, are being transformed into the same image from glory to glory, just as by the Spirit of the Lord."

(2 Corinthians 3:18 NKJV)

"You Can Only Do So Much"

That's right. And we seldom do. This is the preferred statement to justify an unwillingness to go even the first mile, let alone the next, with someone who is unlovable. Why do we sometimes feel personally offended or violated by people who are trapped in cycles of self-destruction? Would not our Heavenly Father have every right to just as quickly give up on us? Some people are seemingly afraid to get a little of the world's dirt on their hands for fear that other people will see it. Isn't that what Jesus did in His earthly ministry? Can you imagine Jesus refusing to hang out with tax collectors and sinners and saying, with a deep sigh, "Well, you can only do so much"? Maybe if we set out to invest ourselves in those who have made poor choices, we would have opportunity to lead them to Christ; you know, grow the Church. There are those who will trample on your pearls. Not everyone we take the time for will have a desire to change, and I get that, but how will we ever be someone's answer to prayer if we let past experiences dictate future ventures of faith?

So, what do you think would happen...if church people walked their talk? The words that come from our lips are important. Not only do they affect others' actions, they affect our own, because the first person to hear our words is us! The word of faith, according to Romans 10, is sufficient to save upon our verbal testimony of Christ. James tells us that it is wise to be slow to speak, but quick to hear. Jesus said that out of the abundance of the heart, the mouth speaks, and that our words can either justify us or condemn us. For the follower of Jesus, what proceeds from our mouths ultimately betrays our hearts. Our words can either fuel our walk of faith, or they can make vain excuses for *not* walking beyond our natural abilities. Which heart attitude do you think God will bless?

CHAPTER TWO

...if the Church Would Tear Down her Idols?

> *"In the eighth year of his reign, while he was still young, he began to seek the God of his father David. In his twelfth year he began to purge Judah and Jerusalem of high places, Asherah poles and idols."*
>
> *(2 Chronicles 34:3 NIV)*

Please allow a bit of science fiction here for the purpose of illustration. Suppose an alien from beyond our galaxy came to earth and eventually, made his way to the United States. While we're supposing, let's say this creature logged on to social media in his desire to learn about our culture. While doing so, he came across one of the many heated discussions regarding the state of Christianity in America today. Without any further information, this visitor from outer space would likely believe that everything in our society was perfect until about 50 years ago! Back then, most people went to church, and everyone who went to church passionately followed Jesus. The government was honest and true, and politicians never lied. Finally, our nation's streets were safe, and all children obeyed their parents.

I am obviously stretching things a bit, and not just the part about the other-worldly visitor, but it's true that many church people have selective amnesia when it comes to failures of the past; that's one thing about memory – it's selective! It enables us, if we so choose, to easily find someone else to blame for the current conditions in society. The truth is, rebellion against God is nothing new in the history of mankind. In fact, there have been fewer good days than bad. That shouldn't make us tolerant of that which is evil, but it should remind us about just how patient, loving, and forgiving our Heavenly Father is! Let's take a trip back in time to the Southern Kingdom of Judah during the time approaching the destruction of Jerusalem and the captivity of its residents by Babylon under King Nebuchadnezzar.

When you look at the history of the Kings of Israel, both of the United Kingdom and the Divided Kingdom, there were a total of 43 rulers. Out of these, only 11 did anything to honor God at all; out of those 11, only 7 were considered to be godly. The one king who stands out head and shoulders above them all was King Josiah of Judah (2 Kings 21-23 and 1 Chronicles 34-35).

Josiah was a true reformer at a time when the nation of Judah desperately needed one! His name, specifically, appears in a prophecy about his reign 350 years before he became king (1 Kings 13:2). 2 Kings 22:2 and 2 Chronicles 34:2 both say, "He did what was right in the eyes of the Lord and walked in the ways of his father David, not turning aside to the right or the left." Of no other king in Israel's history was it written that he did not turn aside to the right or the left. He stands alone in the pages of Bible history as one who did what was right from beginning to end (2 Kings 23:25). There were other kings who made noble efforts toward purging the nation of pagan worship, but Josiah's efforts were all-inclusive. His reforms went even beyond the borders of Judah into the regions of the former northern kingdom of Israel, removing all the *high places* erected by former kings.

Josiah's reforms brought results. While repairs to the Temple were being made, the Passover was reinstituted. Most scholars agree that the book of Deuteronomy was discovered then. As long as Josiah lived, the people were faithful to follow the Lord. Unfortunately for Judah, however, they returned to their old ways of disobedience under subsequent kings. When they did so, they were recipients of God's judgement; Jerusalem was destroyed, and the Jews were carried into captivity by the Babylonians. Even though Josiah died 35 years earlier and was spared the agony of seeing the day of Judah's calamity, God's promise of judgment came to pass.

The accounts of the reign of good King Josiah found in God's Word are more than just historical facts about God's people, Israel. They also stand as a warning for the Church, a warning that shows that unless we are cognizant of our *own* idols and high places, and promptly set out to destroy them, we are just as deserving of judgement as ancient Judah. Many church people fail to recognize even the *existence* of such, much less desire to do anything about them! The truth is, although there are not obvious physical idols and altars to false gods littering the American landscape today, *idolatry* is high on the list of pet sins of the church. If idolatry is anything that takes the place of God, or keeps us from serving God, it stands to reason that idols don't have to be physical objects made of stone or wood. Actually, it's the *non-tangible* ones that are the most destructive.

Following up on the sci-fi analogy of the visitor from outer space, I believe that, in response to a dramatic shift in pop culture in recent history, some Christians have confused *memory* for *doctrine*; the *"good old days"* for *Scripture*, and *personal preference* for a *genuine relationship with God* through Jesus Christ. The idols of memory, the "good old days," and personal preference are in reality idols of *self*. They must be destroyed.

The Idols of Memory and the "Good Old Days"

The memory of days gone by, when no one questioned the authority of the Bible or the existence of God, and daily life looked like Mayberry, North Carolina, on *The Andy Griffith Show*, is a myth. Because our society is so rapidly changing and shifting, it seems by comparison that there once indeed *was* a time when everything was perfect and sublime. That type of selective memory soon becomes an idol to a god that doesn't exist and never has! In fact, the very notion of the "good old days" becomes a hinderance to what God wants to do in and though us in the future!

I have met Christians who have adopted a defeated attitude about this world that has really become their *doctrine*. Because of this, they've become spiritually lazy and shifted into preservation mode. "I'm just hanging on until Jesus comes," they say. It's un-Biblical; it's un-Christlike; it's faithless. It's a slap in the face of the Holy Spirit who hasn't changed with the times like we have. The indwelling, empowering, enabling Holy Spirit still fills and changes and transforms and employs Christians who yield to His control. A defeated attitude arising from idols of memory and the "good old days" is blatantly un-Scriptural. It seems obvious to me that many of the original apostles believed that Christ was returning during their lifetime. In spite of this, yet they would not be defeated; they served Jesus until their dying breaths. How ironic it is that those who claim superior knowledge of the Scriptures are so often the very ones who ignore it for the sake of memories of days that never were!

Listen, I'm sixty years old, and that's plenty of time to have developed selective memories of a time when everything was better. Trust me, there are times when I want to move to a cabin in the woods and generate my own electricity, grow vegetables, tune out the outside world, and just simplify. But here's the thing: I want to make a difference in a world that is becoming increasingly secular and vulgar towards all things sacred, and I can't use the past as an excuse to miss the future that God wants to build through Spirit-filled Christians willing to tear down their idols of memory for the sake of those who don't yet know Christ! The idols of memory only serve to make us bitter and critical of the future, and therefore not very pliable in the Hands of Almighty God. Make no mistake, there is coming a day of final judgement; there is coming a day when God is going to say, "It's all over, Son, go get My church!" There is coming a day when our work will be over, but I don't know when that day will be and neither does anyone else. It's fair to say that the American church could use some Josiahs, not in leading political reform, but in reformation of heart! *What do you think would happen*, if church people tore down their idols of memory, and believed God for their future?

The Idols of Personal Preference

The sweeping reforms made by King Josiah not only involved *removing* the things that dishonored God, the altars to Baal, the Asherah poles and other abominations, but also *adding* those things which honored God: reinstituting the Passover, renewing the Covenant found in the newly rediscovered Book of the Law, and physically restoring the Temple. Josiah didn't concern himself with the personal preferences of anyone in doing so, because God's commands trumped anyone's preference. Actually, it was the people's personal preferences that got them into trouble in the first place! They traded their relationship with a holy God for their own personal preferences, mainly the worship of other nations' gods that were *not* gods at all! It's easy for us to look with disdain upon their disobedience and shake our heads in bewilderment; how could a people so blessed reject the One true God who had brought them out of bondage into their own prosperous land, for the sake of idols made of wood and stone?

The truth is, many today elevate their personal preferences above the commands of Christ. This error can continue unseen and unchallenged for years, even decades, until brought to light either by the secular world or by Biblically motivated reformers. Both are seen as the enemy by church people who have chosen to defend personal preference over the dictates of Scripture. This happens in both liberal and conservative churches, mainly because the terms "liberal" and "conservative" need to apply to something; the terms don't stand on their own. You can be liberal about theology but conservative about liturgy, and you can be conservative about theology and liberal about liturgy. Interestingly enough, both camps are most threatened by those who mess with their liturgy, although one prints theirs in the bulletin and the other generally does not.

I have described myself many times as a Biblical conservative and a church liberal, meaning I believe the Bible is the absolute, authoritative Word of God, but that we can be creative about the way we "do" church. This statement usually makes the Pharisees scowl, because I dared to even utter the word *liberal.* I have to admit, this brings a sheepish grin to my face.

Everyone is allowed their personal preferences, even within the church. If we were all the same, life would be boring, but if personal preference displaces Almighty God as the center of our worship, then shouldn't we pull down and destroy any such idols of our own personal preference that keep us from being the disciples God has designed us to be? Most of the fights and splits in churches today have more to do with preference than doctrine. A music pastor takes the position that the team will perform no song written before 1998, and the musical preferences of half the congregation are deemed irrelevant, while at the same time, some in the congregation refuse to adapt to newer music, calling it ungodly simply because it isn't found in their favorite hymnbook. A pastor leads an outreach in the community that brings in people who look, dress, and even smell differently and suddenly, the unwritten dress code that everyone is supposed to adhere to is violated. The list goes on. Bible translation, length of the Sunday service, pews versus chairs, and even the color of the paint on the walls of the sanctuary (real issues that have divided churches!) all take the place of Biblical mandates for the church to follow, and therefore become idols of personal preference. "Going to church" has replaced "being the church" in importance. Nowhere in scripture does God say anything about "going to church."

Show me a church that is divided over idols of memory and the "good old days" and personal preference and I'll show you a church that is dying or dead. Some of them need hospice care so they can at least recognize the fact that death is soon to follow. In many cases, closure is the best thing that could happen, for the sake of the Kingdom of God. What if church people determined to have Josiah's heart by removing what is evil, adding what is holy, cultivating a heart of obedience to God, being willing to stand on God's side—even if others fail to follow—all the time, using whatever influence and favor God grants them to lead others to do the same?

What do you think would happen if the local church actually took the time to identify and tear down their idols and replace them with Christlikeness—love for the lost, commitment to holiness, and a genuine desire to be used of God to love one another?

Well, I'll tell you what would happen. We would see genuine, God-sent revival—the kind that comes in response to humble and hungry hearts—the kind that influences culture and society—the kind that "brings back" important things, not memories and sacred cows. We need it. All of us. Revival isn't just something that "the world" needs or that "other people" need. Every believer needs to be revived. Regularly. And nothing is stopping you. Do it.

CHAPTER THREE

...if God's People Would Pray?

"One day Jesus was praying in a certain place. When he finished, one of his disciples said to him, 'Lord, teach us to pray, just as John taught his disciples.'"

(Luke 11:1 NIV)

We *talk* about prayer, we assert that there is *power* in prayer, and we say that we couldn't make it through the day *without* prayer. However, when the opportunity arises for the local body of believers to meet together to pray, most stay home or find something else to do. If we were to boil down the problems of the church in America today to one single issue, it would *have* to be prayerlessness. The Bible speaks more about prayer than preaching, singing, worshipping, or almost any other "churchy" topic you can imagine, yet prayerlessness remains the single most fixable, but neglected, aspect of church life today. In his book, *Fresh Power*, Brooklyn Tabernacle Pastor Jim Cymbala writes:

> One of the distinguishing traits of the early church was their practice of serious prayer. The apostles had never said, "Lord, teach us to preach" or "Lord, teach us to worship." But they had asked, "Lord, teach us to pray..." Something about Jesus' ability to commune with His Father in heaven fascinated them.[22]

For most churches today, the lowest attended corporate worship event is the prayer meeting, if it even exists at all. Many a pastor has sensed God's leading in the area of prayer, only to be thoroughly frustrated by the lack of participation from the congregation. Excuses made by mostly holier-than-thou church members about why they can't take part are almost laughable. Soon, the whole emphasis stalls, stamped "dead on arrival," before it can even get traction. Meanwhile, the SMOs (Sunday Morning Onlys) whine and complain about the degradation of society and the absence of moral values in the schools—along with a litany of other gripes that would be best taken to God in prayer.

> "But when you pray, go into your room and shut the door and pray to your Father who is in secret. And your Father who sees in secret will reward you."
>
> (Jesus Christ, in Matthew 6:6 ESV)

Let's get one thing settled: public prayer does not replace private prayer. Just because you show up at a prayer meeting at your church doesn't mean you pray, does it? Jesus had something to say about private prayer. He called it "prayer closet" kind of praying—the kind no one sees but you and God. However, if you are a private prayer, shouldn't you also be a public prayer? If it's valuable in the prayer closet, why isn't it valuable in public places with other believers? Jesus' admonition in Matthew 6:6 is not that we shouldn't pray together in public, but that we are not to pray in public to be seen as spiritually superior to others, as was the case of the religious Jews of His day. I will be so bold as to go on record as saying those who fail to engage in prayer with other believers, by and large, neglect private prayer time as well.

So…why is this? How can the activity of prayer be viewed as most important and least important all at the same time? Why do so many people invest *more* time *avoiding* praying than actually *doing* it? It *must* be either selfishness or unbelief; why else would people who identify as Christ-followers not want to pursue Him in intimate conversation? What else could explain the drastic decrease in participation from Sunday morning worship to the corporate prayer service, *whenever* it's held? Let's examine these motives.

Selfishness

People have been told for decades, especially in our American culture, that *self* is the most important thing, and we are to, "Look out for number one." With that in mind, it's no surprise that many believe it, even church people! *Self* is the enemy of intercessory prayer. *Self* is content to stay home or find something more entertaining than a boring old prayer meeting. *Self* sees no value in praying with other believers for some*thing* or some*one* other than—you guessed it—*self*!

E.M. Bounds was a nineteenth century pastor and author who is perhaps best known for his book, *Power Through Prayer*. Those who knew Bounds personally have testified of his unrelenting devotion to prayer; it is said of him that he prayed for three hours each morning before even considering proceeding to his work. There's a marvelous quote attributed to him that expresses the beauty of intercessory prayer:

> Talking to men for God is a great thing, but talking to God for men is greater still. He will never talk well and with real success to men for God who has not learned well how to talk to God for men.[33]

If self is the enemy of intercessory prayer, the inverse must also be true—that intercessory prayer is the enemy of self. The exercise itself forces the petitioner to focus not on himself, but on others. When that is done in a public setting with other believers, we are, in a sense, guarded from slipping into self. If Christians made a practice of praying for others, their priorities would shift, their hearts would mature, their passions would move outward, and interestingly enough, their own needs would be met, as others of like-mindedness in prayer would be simultaneously praying for them.

We do live in a selfish society. There is good news, however, as data seems to indicate that the millennial generation is actually reversing this trend. I know...I know...Millennials have been called the "me" generation, self-absorbed and narcissistic but it seems that as they age (the oldest millennials turn 43 in 2024), they are becoming *less* selfish and *more* generous. According to an October 2021 report from The Barna Institute, not only are millennials more secure in their talents and abilities, 67% of them are motivated to be generous with others in using their skills. That's a full ten percentage points *higher* than their elder generation, the boomers![44] Additionally, according to a blog published on tithe.ly, millennial Christians are the most likely of all age groups to say that generosity is most important to them personally.[55] This is a step in the right direction—after all, there can be no greater example of selflessness than Christ Himself, "w*ho, existing in the form of God, did not consider equality with God as something to be exploited." (Philippians 2:6 CSB)*

What do you think would happen, if Christians recognized and surrendered their selfishness in the area of prayer? *What do you think would happen*, if church people asked God to take away their excuses for neglecting their single greatest blessing—prayer?

Unbelief

I think this is one area where the simple answer is largely ignored either because it's too simple or too offensive. To tell someone the reason they aren't praying is because of their unbelief is not a way to win friends and influence parishioners, but it just *has* to be true! Can I use the pronoun "you" for a while? It's not personal…unless it is.

If you truly believed that God hears and answers prayer, why would you not rush to do it? If you truly believed that prayer is the means by which mankind has an audience with the King of the universe, why would there be such a long list of other more important duties ahead of it? If you had a choice of attending a worship service, a potluck dinner, or a prayer meeting, why would the latter be on the bottom of the list? I can tell you why; it's because of unbelief! The worship service is a given, because, well, it's Sunday morning, and you *have* to go to church on Sunday morning, because if you don't, someone will call you out on it. The potluck dinner is a necessity because church people love "fellowship," but the prayer meeting? Eh, it's only the prayer meeting—what could you miss by avoiding that? You *believe* that Sunday morning is important; kind of like a bare minimum requirement. You *believe* the potluck is important because, well, let's get serious; you love to eat, but you *don't believe* the prayer meeting is important because, deep down, you don't *really believe* what you say about prayer!

If you were chosen to have a meeting with the President of the United States, you would clear your schedule to make room. Even if the President were to hear you, there's no guarantee that he would answer you. God does both, if you'd give Him the opportunity! The barometer of success for the institutionalized church today is Sunday morning attendance in the building with pews or chairs, all looking one way. Why? Show me chapter and verse why that should be so. The most important event in the life of the church should be meeting together to pray with and for one another, to know God more completely, and to place ourselves on the altar, crying out, "Lord, use me!" Instead, because of unbelief, many church people go through religious motions, but never order their lives to respect the priorities that Jesus taught and followed Himself! The simple answer is—unbelief. The same could be applied to trusting God, taking God at His Word, being used in the Gifts of the Spirit, letting the Holy Spirit continue to transform us, and more!

What do you think would happen, if Christians actually believed what they *claim* to believe about prayer, and put that belief into action? If Jesus, being fully God, deemed it necessary to pray, how can we neglect it and still be considered His disciples? *What do you think would happen* to the level of influence the Church would have in society today if proclaiming disciples followed the example of their Rabbi and placed prayer in its rightful place in their lives?

Prayer, private and public equally, shapes the lives of believers and the vision of the local church. No church program or good work can rival the spiritual productivity of a child of God on his or her knees. Prayer doesn't simply petition God to act on our behalf; it allows God to petition *us* to act on *His* behalf, and to be conformed more and more to the image of His Son. When I think of the popular phrase "Prayer Changes Things," I'm more and more convinced that prayer changes *me* more than the things around me. *What do you think would happen*, if we truly allowed the Lord to teach us to pray?

"But I Don't Know How!"

I'm amazed at the number of regular church attenders who *think* they don't know how to pray. Ask someone to lead out in prayer at a church gathering of almost any "brand," and you'll unfortunately find those who feign humility by declining to pray. Public prayer with other believers should not be a burden, nor should it be a forum to try to impress others with eloquence. Praying aloud in a small group setting with other believers is a treasured experience—one that should be often repeated. Given half a chance, the Holy Spirit will descend with love and grace in such a setting, confirming Himself in ways which can only be described as miraculous. I fear that our greatest asset has been misunderstood as the greatest fear of some—praying out loud in front of others. What a pity! If you know how to pray in private, you know how to pray in public. Superstars and showboats need not apply, only those who recognize the immense privilege we have as God's children not only to pray in Jesus' name, but to pray with fellow believers! *What do you think would happen*, if local churches all over the world approached the prayer meeting with the same vigor as they approach the potluck dinner? I don't have to be a prophet to *know* what would happen: believers would be encouraged, the body of Christ would grow closer together, the needs of the individual members of the church would be met, and God would move in response to the *effectual fervent prayers* of the saints! Come on, Church—get over your collective selfishness and unbelief and commit yourselves anew to the single greatest privilege we have: prayer!

CHAPTER FOUR

...if God's People Truly Sought Revival?

It is said that English is one of the most difficult languages to learn as a second language, in part because of the varied meanings of words that are spelled the same **yet** have entirely different meanings. Both trees and dogs have "bark." You can "mine" for gold and when you find some, declare, "This is mine." If you're not careful when you are weeding your garden, you can "squash" your "squash," and sometimes, people hit the wrong "nail" when using a hammer.

Sometimes, the meaning of a word with numerous and varied definitions can be cheapened. Take for example, the word "love." I can love lasagna, I can love summertime, I can love my spouse and my family, and I can love God—but the love I feel for each is very different. So often, the word "love" is used indiscriminately, especially when expressing love for one other or love of God. To apply the same weight of meaning to my love for my wife as I assign to my love of ice cream would be ridiculous.

Some church people toss around churchy words independent of context, thereby cheapening their meaning. Not only can our improperly used lexicon be confusing to those outside the walls of the church, it can also improperly inform and motivate those on the inside. One such "religious" term that is in dire need of re-defining is the word "revival."

In 2002, I was leading worship for a family camp in the Northern Midwest and had the privilege of sitting under the ministry of Dr. Gordon Anderson. At the time, he was president of North Central University in Minneapolis. On one of the nights that he was speaking—I think it was the first—Dr. Anderson made a statement that I have remembered and long "borrowed." He said that in order to be revived, you have to have been "vived" in the first place! I suppose deep down I knew that to be true, but it took this moment in my life to truly comprehend what genuine revival really is. As far as the Church is concerned, it's God making us alive again! That means, we had to have been made alive in the first place! Something that has never been alive cannot be revived! Revival is truly, in the most literal definition of the word, for the *Church* and furthermore, for the individual members *of* the Church—*all* of them! Of course, there are a few people who don't agree with that.

"Revival is for everyone else except me."

Some church people talk about "revival" as if it's something that everyone *else* needs. Like a rain cloud, revival hovers over a specific church, town, or nation and soon the rain falls, landing only, of course, on "those sinners" who are far from God. Along with the rain of revival comes the "old-time way." I'm not sure how everyone's "old-time way" comes at the same time, but apparently, this is how God works. In this imaginary scenario, all of the problems of said church, town or nation are immediately solved, mainly, because everyone adopts the same point of view as the one who is praying for revival. Again, I'm not sure how that works; I guess I'm one of the backslidden. To complete this ridiculous fantasy, revival also causes all our politicians—at least, the ones we voted for—to become believers in Jesus. In this misunderstanding of revival, you'll know when revival has truly arrived when the bars close, the jails are empty, and the adult bookstores close.

Think I'm overdoing it? Maybe. But, then again, you haven't had the conversations I've had with some self-righteous church people who arrogantly believe that if Jesus were to appear on earth today, He would think like them, live like them, and vote like them. They call out loudly for revival yet do nothing to personally prepare for it. Their attitude is actually anti-revival; it's an attitude that assumes they have the mind of Christ in all things and could not *possibly* be in need of correction from God. How tragic! The truth is, genuine revival comes as saints recognize their *own* desperate need for more of God. It's a need to be forgiven, made holy, transformed, filled with the Holy Spirit, *re-filled* with the Holy Spirit, challenged, and empowered to be all that God wants them to be. It's for His honor and glory beyond their cherished memories of days gone by and their biased personal preferences.

Genuine revival is personal and inconvenient. Truth is, it rarely comes like anyone expects! It causes believers to take an honest internal spiritual inventory and then *do* something about it! Heaven-sent revival comes in answer to a contrite heart, one that can be broken and remade in the image of the Son. Interestingly enough, revival comes personally to a believer who desires to be hungry for God, as well as one who already is! Maybe you've never been there, but I have; I go through occasional times when I want to be hungry for God, but just feel cold and empty. I also experience times when I'm so hungry, I just want to see what's over the next hill, spiritually speaking, but just can't seem to. Sometimes this happens in the same 24-hour period! The great thing is, *being* hungry and *wanting to be hungry* are both great positions to be in before a loving Heavenly Father who desperately desires to invest Himself in His children.

Two Parts to Revival

There are two parts to genuine revival. First, it comes individually for every believer who assumes the proper position of being humble and contrite before a holy God. Secondly, it comes corporately in the sense that personal revival spreads supernaturally from one energized disciple to another. In the larger passage of scripture from 1 Corinthians 12, the Apostle Paul explains how believers in Jesus are to work together as one unit using the analogy of the human body. Verse 26 says, "If one part suffers, every part suffers with it; if one part is honored, every part rejoices with it." (1 Corinthians 12:26, NIV) Every influence in the body of Christ, whether good or bad, affects the whole body.

It's easy to see how this is true in the negative by observing the rapid growth of strife and division in the church. I ministered in a town once at Second Baptist Church; you guessed it—right down the street from First Baptist Church. *What do you think would happen* if the second part of that verse, "if one part is honored, every part rejoices with it," were true on a large scale? *What do you think would happen* if every Christian honored the body of Christ by personally honoring God? There's just no earthly limit to the potential growth of the Kingdom of God when the church takes its responsibility seriously!

I'm thankful that we have record of genuine moves of God—revivals that reached the masses—so that we can look at what preceded and proceeded them. Space will not allow me to go into detail on each, and besides, there is no shortage of books already written about them. I heartily recommend seeking these out; they allow a far-removed, big-picture perspective that is invaluable for the modern investigator. Interestingly, the Bible doesn't say much about revival apart from that of the nation of Israel. It does, however, warn us from beginning to end about staying true to the Lord and not turning away from Him and to our own self-will. A good Bible study for introspection is found in the first three chapters of the book of Revelation. The letters to the seven churches in the province of Asia, dictated by Jesus and written down by John, are a must-read for the seeker of personal and corporate revival today. There are other resources as well that can give you a taste of the miraculous, such as the *God's Generals* series of books by Roberts Liardon. Liardon gives the good and the bad—successes and failures—of ordinary men and women who were miraculously used in genuine moves of God throughout world history. I've read them all a couple of times each, and they never fail to encourage me to trust God for the miraculous. If you're feeling dry and dead and want to be hungry, I heartily recommend these books.[6]

Another classic read is *Why Revival Tarries,* written by Leonard Ravenhill. Although written in the mid 1950's, this book is timeless. I've read it myself many times, and I will read it again, I'm sure. There is also a very good revival website at www.revivalradiotv.com that is a great resource for the student of revival history. Of course, with any study of history, we shouldn't try to replicate the past. History never exactly repeats itself. However, if we can understand the heart attitudes of those whom God used in the past, we can better understand how our attitudes need to be adjusted to come into agreement with the Lord. *What do you think would happen*, if believers in Christ would allow God to adjust our attitudes about revival? What are some attitudes that may need to be adjusted? Here are a few.

"I'm just holding on until the rapture."

Leonard Ravenhill used to say, "Some people want to be raptured from responsibility."[7] In other words, "Lord, take me out of here so I don't have to do what You've asked me to do." This just can't be! While we know that our true home is not of this world, the church cannot simply give up, coast, and await the rapture! I can't imagine standing before God someday, having ignored His call upon my life, and giving the excuse, "I thought the rapture was coming in my lifetime, so I didn't do anything for You." God forbid our longing for heaven becomes an excuse for laziness!

John 9:4 KJV reads, "I must work the works of him that sent me, while it is day: the night cometh, when no man can work." In context, Jesus uttered this truth just before healing a man born blind. The night, for Jesus, would come when His earthly life was complete. For us, night could come at death, or when our opportunities for ministry come to an end for some other reason. Our night will also come when Jesus returns to catch away His Church! At that time, our earthly ministry will cease, but until then, we need to keep serving the Lord as if the night will never come! Work while it is still day! Don't go to bed early! Continue to pray for revival and believe God for the miraculous! *What do you think would happen*, if God's responsibility-avoiding, rapture-awaiting servants came out of retirement and joined the ranks of the employed in making a difference for the Kingdom of God?

"What can I do? I'm only one person."

Every genuine move of God began with a willing vessel, usually unknown at the time and *always* humble before God. From the Biblical apostles to present day champions of the faith, God has always chosen ordinary men and women to do extraordinary things for His glory! Although history sometimes remembers these willing vessels as celebrities, they don't start out that way; God transforms unknown, humble, and hungry servants into anointed leaders who influence their churches, communities, and nations for Christ! They were "only one person" when they said, "yes" to the Holy Spirit. Why can't we do the same? We don't have to know the end from the beginning. Only God knows that. However, we can simply put one foot in front of the other, in faith and obedience, and trust God to do the rest.

What do you think would happen, if every believer saw themselves as potential leaders (the way God sees them) and rose to the challenge of obedience, trusting not in their own talents, but in the God who gives gifts generously to those who have a heart after Him? The road to influence in the Kingdom of God has many curves, hills, and valleys. Personal sacrifice is the toll, and humility before God is the essential vehicle of the journey, but the benefits of obedience, at the end of the road, far outweigh the price of the trip.

"The world is too far gone for revival."

If your loved one were given a terminal diagnosis, would you acquiesce to the threat of the disease, or would you do everything in your power—and God's power—to eradicate it? Easy answer; of course, you would exhaust every means of finding a cure. Why are some people so willing to give up on a sick society, especially one whose remedy is as close as our knees? It's as if they don't believe God is able to transform a culture that has turned its back on Him. Perhaps some who take this stance fail to rely on God's power because they're only thinking in terms of human solutions. Politics, the entertainment business, and the world's financial systems have *nothing* on the supernatural power of God! The strongholds of the enemy, though significant, cannot overshadow the power of a Holy God. The same power that can transform an ugly human heart can transform a nation's ugliness into something beautiful. The world has been in deplorable circumstances before, only to have genuine revival restore its prospects. The truth is, it's not *our call* to say when "the world is too far gone for revival." That's up to God. We live in a day and age when hopeless people are looking for hope in pursuits that aren't built to *contain* hope. If God's own children have no hope to offer them, why should they ever look to the One who can give them a brand new, hope-filled eternal existence that starts right now? If you are convinced there's no hope for a dying world, exactly *whose* power are you relying on?

What do you think would happen, if the church stopped placing human limitations on God? *What do you think would happen*, if believers who claim to be people of prayer lived that out beyond religious-sounding lip service? *What do you think would happen,* if Christians would bombard heaven for *spiritual* revival as desperately as they lobby Washington D.C. for *legislative* revival? History testifies that God would answer such a plea! Why would He not? I'm not suggesting we approach revival like a recipe, or that we portend to define and predict a sovereign move of God. However, knowing God's unchanging character, why would He refuse to answer the earnest cry of humble hearts who desperately want to see God glorified and exalted among His people on earth? Are we weeping for the state of our churches, our communities, our nation, and our earth, or have we grown cold and insensitive to the overwhelming decadence of a godless society? May it never be!

What do you think would happen, if the church got serious about seeking genuine personal and corporate revival even against perceived negative odds? I believe the answer to the question is an easy one: God would move once again in His churches, and Christians would have multiple new testimonies to share with their friends and family. I believe many people would find Jesus irresistible as a result, and society would experience a moral upswing, even among those who do not come to Christ, simply because a larger constituency's lifestyle demands it. This is how Church is *supposed* to influence culture—by their example, not by legislation—and it *should* be happening today!

CHAPTER FIVE

...if the Anti-Church Figured Out What It's For?

"Do everything without complaining and arguing, so that no one can criticize you.

Live clean, innocent lives as children of God, shining like bright lights in a world full of crooked and perverse people."

(Philippians 2:14-15 NLT)

"Be hospitable to one another without grumbling."

(1 Peter 4:9 NKJV)

If you took time to read the above scriptures, you may have deduced that "The Anti-Church" is not about those who are against the Church, but instead, it is the churches that seem to be against everything—while knowing little of what they're actually *for*! These churches both attract and are comprised of those who seldom smile and are self-appointed joy-killers. I admit, I have little patience in dealing with those whose strongly negative personalities suck all the victory out of the room.

The pastor doesn't preach right, the worship songs are all wrong, the kids are disrespectful, and most everyone they know is not following Jesus. Of course, the accusers are guiltless; it's everyone *else's* fault that things are the way they are!

I'm sorry if I've depressed you by bringing up memories of negative church experiences and people who have looked down their hypercritical noses at you; I've been on the receiving end of those stares too, so I know what it's like! I feel no hate for them. I only feel sorrow that they somehow think they aren't standing for Jesus unless they're railing against everyone else. It takes a special combination of patience and honesty to deal effectively with such people. I think most people, including pastors, would just as soon bypass them completely when they come into the building with pews and a steeple.

We humans have reasons for everything we do. There is a foundation, a motive, for every thought, word, and deed that we produce. Granted, the motivations might exist only in the subconscious, but they exist just the same. Jesus knew this and was very good at dragging motives—especially improper ones—out of the subconscious and into the light of day. This can be clearly seen in the gospels where Jesus challenged the statements, beliefs, and practices of the religious Jews of His day. Whenever you read these accounts, I encourage you to ask questions:

> Why did Jesus answer their question with a question?
> Why did Jesus' statement make them so angry?
> Why couldn't they answer Jesus' question?
> Why was Jesus such a threat to them?

The answer? *Jesus identified their selfish, ungodly motives.* No one had ever done this the way Jesus did, because He was God in the flesh! He knew their motives better than they did! They didn't like being outed; they didn't appreciate being made to look foolish; Jesus messed with their old-time religion! The religious leaders of Jesus' day who challenged Him on every side did so out of jealousy and the threat of losing their positions of influence. They wanted no one to upset the status quo, lest Rome see their religion as a threat to its Empire. Ironically, about forty years after Jesus' earthly ministry, that's *exactly* what happened when the Temple and the city of Jerusalem were destroyed by the Roman army.

What about the "blame everyone for everything" crowd that comprises the Anti-Church today? What motivates their negative knee-jerk reaction to anything that falls outside of their religious purview? Why do they perceive their condemnation of all things unfamiliar as a good and righteous act? What do you think it would take to turn this segment of Church people around? What do you think would happen if this reversal were successful?

This may be a good time to pause and establish some parameters for this line of thought; this is the best way to avoid misunderstanding. As a matter of fact, I believe most fights in the church today (and perhaps even in politics) could be avoided if the "sides" more clearly understood one another's foundational positions. I do not propose that everything new and improved in the area of how we "do church" is good. We do well to stand and not be swayed by pop culture, wolves in sheep's clothing, or even our emotions. Ephesians 4:14 describes the fruit of Christian maturity:

> "Then we will no longer be infants, tossed back and forth by the waves, and blown here and there by every wind of teaching and by the cunning and craftiness of people in their scheming."
>
> (Ephesians 4:14 NIV)

There are hills worth fighting for, but many church people mistake molehills for mountains out of a deep-seated desire to resist change and preserve the status quo at all costs. Beneath this resistance to change is a root motivation that upon first glance may seem to be a stand for authenticity and orthodoxy, but upon deeper excavation, the true motivation comes to light. *Most people like to be comfortable, and any threat to that comfort earns a negative reaction*. In many cases, the *greatest* resistance to change occurs when non-Biblical standards are violated! In these instances, those who resist *think* they are standing on Biblical grounds when in fact, only their personal preferences are being defended. Chalk one up for Biblical illiteracy masquerading as spiritual maturity.

The funny thing is that many people refuse to change, even if they're not happy where they are presently. Although they may not like their current circumstances, they are at least familiar, and there's a degree of comfort in familiarity. There's also death in that, spiritually speaking. Jesus' own words prove this in His conversations with the Jewish leaders:

> "You search the Scriptures because you think they give you eternal life. But the Scriptures point to me!"
>
> (John 5:39 NLT)

The motivations of the Jewish leaders were comfort and sustainability ***of*** comfort; they were expecting Messiah to come, but they had convinced themselves what Messiah would be like when He came, and Jesus didn't look like what they expected! So, rather than changing their traditions, they sought to eliminate the One who was disturbing the familiar, even when the very scriptures they were searching testified of Him! Some people do that today; they will search the scriptures looking for a single verse to justify their belligerence, rather than allowing their comfortable, familiar ways of thinking to be disrupted by the God who is always leading us forward, not backward.

A local church can become so *anti-everything* they become unified in their antagonism, but it's a false unity. From the inside looking out, its members think they are united against the world, but from the outside looking in, they're becoming a cult. The Anti-Church has convinced itself that it is taking a unified stand for God when, in fact, it has only taken a unified stand for its own way of doing things. The Church is comprised of all true believers in Jesus Christ and must therefore work together to achieve Christ's mandate of going into all the world and making disciples. The Church, capital "C," is the one Jesus gave Himself for; He didn't live, die, defeat death, ascend and send His Holy Spirit so that exclusive clubs could form and blame the unbelieving world for its fear and complacency. Salvation is free, but following Jesus is costly, especially in terms of comfort zones. Being a disciple of Jesus is not achieved by hiding *from* the world, but by being *in* the world, yet not *of* it.

What do you think would happen if church people evaluated "new things" according to the trinity of scripture, prayer, and the leading of the Holy Spirit? How many artificial barriers of age, culture, tradition, race, and language might disappear if, before Christians instantly erected stop signs, they yielded to the illumination of the Spirit? How much harmful, divisive rhetoric would be avoided if those who claim to follow Christ would seek to identify the foundation of their negative reactions before opening their mouths in stubborn defiance to the will of God?

I love the closing verses of the book of Job when Job has an "aha" moment. It is written of this man, in the opening verse of the book that bears his name, that he "was blameless and upright; he feared God and shunned evil." (Job 1:1b NIV) How would you like that to be written of you? I can think of no greater tribute. If you've read the book of Job, you know that, in spite of his upright character and his stellar witness, Job endures horrific trials as Satan is allowed to inflict him with personal loss far beyond anything that most of us have ever experienced. In addition, his "friends" tell him that God would never allow this to happen to him unless Job had done something terrible, and they urge him to repent. Job doesn't realize that the source of his trials is Satan, and he insists that he's done nothing deserving of punishment, which was true—but there is *one thing* that he eventually confesses to God, and that is written in Chapter 42, verses 2 and 3:

> *"I know that you can do all things; no purpose of yours can be thwarted. You asked, 'Who is this that obscures my plans without knowledge?' Surely I spoke of things I did not understand, things too wonderful for me to know."*
>
> *(Job 42:2-3 NIV)*

Job questioned God and incorrectly reacted to what was happening to him by speaking of things he did not understand. He did not understand that his trial was not a punishment, but an opportunity for God to be glorified even in disastrous circumstances. While Job passed the test, he had to humble himself before God and admit his stubbornness. God eventually blessed Job and restored his fortunes—and then some! The closing verses tell us that God blessed Job in the latter part of his life even more than the former.

While the context of Job's story is different than the theme of this chapter, the humble statement that Job made before God can be applied to church people today when they engage their mouths before understanding the whole story! How much personal damage is done to sincere followers of Jesus who are immediately dismissed because their road to the cross looks different than others! How dare we presume our experiences upon others who come to Jesus from a different lifestyle or culture? What difference does it make if their sins are different than ours? Wherever sinners come from, the cross is the desired and only viable destination!

Just like the Pharisees of Jesus' day, the Pharisees in the *Anti-Church* of today are often jealous of the blessings they see in other congregations, especially the ones which are making a difference in the Kingdom of God. Jealousy of a larger church by a smaller Anti-Church gets "spiritualized" with the attitude, "Well, we may be small, but at least we're not like *THAT* church!" A church isn't better because it is bigger, but it's not better because it's smaller, either! Most Anti-Churches are small churches which see a church of any size as apostate—not because they actually are, but because they *must* be, or else they wouldn't be successful!

I have seen so much of this nonsense over the years that I'm sick to my stomach just thinking about it. After all, the fact that a local church has chairs instead of pews, a table instead of a pulpit, and a rocking worship band instead of an organ is *not* reason enough to suspect that the doctrine espoused there is of the devil, and the pastor is Antichrist in the flesh! Jealousy is an ugly thing, especially when attempting to cover it with religious garments.

Consider the blessings in the form of people that may be overlooked by a local congregation which is against everything and everyone that doesn't look like them, namely, the giftings, talents and testimonies of redeemed people that could enrich and inspire its members to greater experience in Christ, the understanding of their varied life journeys and experiences, the education gleaned from other races and cultures which enable a local body of believers to reach out to entirely new people groups, and the list goes on.

What do you think would happen, if grumpy Christians got a fresh dose of the joy of the Lord by opening themselves up to people who have traveled a different path to Jesus? What do you think would happen if the naysayers made it a point to connect with people who worship differently? This is not to have anyone's preferences diminished, but to appreciate the vast love of God. His love, thankfully, transcends human traditions and cleanses hearts—all kinds of hearts—which have been blackened by sin. The unbelieving world has a pretty good idea what the church is against. Isn't it time that they realize what we're for?

CHAPTER SIX

...if the American Church Got its Politics in Perspective?

> "That Sunday evening the disciples were meeting behind locked doors because they were afraid of the Jewish leaders. Suddenly, Jesus was standing there among them! 'Peace be with you,' he said."
>
> (John 20:19 NLT)

The early church was persecuted from day one. During Easter evening, the first "Sunday evening service," the disciples were together in a room with the door securely barred. They were all afraid of what might happen to them, either at the hands of the religious leaders or the Roman officials who were occupying Jerusalem to keep the peace. The news of Jesus' resurrection was spreading like wildfire, although the Jews had bribed the guards to lie about His body's disappearance from the sealed tomb. If anyone had a right to be afraid, it was the ones who were known associates of the Nazarene Rabbi who had caused such division among the people.

It was into this fearful, emotionally charged atmosphere that the risen Christ made His entrance—unhindered by locked doors. The first thing He said to His disciples was, "Peace to you." Jesus displayed His wounds for all to see, and said, "As the Father has sent Me, I also send you." (John 20:21 NKJV)

The fact that their beloved Teacher was once again in their presence must have been surreal to these already frightened followers. Can you just imagine being a first-hand witness of Jesus, alive again in His glorified body? Their minds surely could not comprehend it all just then; they had never experienced anything like this before! Yet, during their shock, Jesus spoke, "Peace to you." He assured them they would be sent into the world, just as He had been. They, indeed, *were* sent just fifty days later. It was on the Day of Pentecost when the Holy Spirit came upon the one hundred twenty in the Upper Room and filled them with power for service.

Not once in Jesus' earthly ministry—either before or after His crucifixion and resurrection—did He promise His followers that the leaders of the government would be their allies. Just before His bodily ascension, Jesus told them to wait for the promise of the Father, the Holy Spirit. He also told them that when the Spirit *did* come, they would receive power to be His witnesses. *Not once* did He tell them that they would have favor with earthly governments, religious or secular, or that they should wait for the promise of a Christian Caesar. If they had waited for Rome's approval, they would never have left Jerusalem!

Why then, today, do so many church people feel they can't "go into all the world and make disciples" until the United States government affirms their beliefs and legislates favor toward the Church? Why, in some cases, has the American flag become so tightly wrapped around the cross of Christ that you often can't tell where politics ends and faith begins? People on both sides of the political aisle try to "claim Jesus," asserting that if He walked the earth today, He would most certainly align with their camp and vote their way. The parties (Pharisees and Sadducees) of Jesus' day tried to get Him to conform too, but He refused to be aligned with either. Would He not do the same in our American political system were He walking the earth today? Of course, He would.

I love the United States of America. I believe that God has blessed this nation because its founding was, in large part, based on Christian principles and values. I cherish our freedoms, believe that personal liberty and responsibility are pillars of the American way of life, and that God indeed wants all people to be free! But it seems to me that our American Church, in many cases, has gone a bit overboard with the idea that America is a "Christian" nation, and therefore, patriotism equals following Jesus.

Don't burn this book just yet. Hear me out. The word "Christian" is not an adjective, as much as it is used that way. After all, we have *Christian* music, *Christian* apparel, *Christian* bookstores, *Christian* dating, *Christian* weddings, *Christian* funerals, and *Christian* almost-anything-else-you-can-think-of. Fact is, the word "Christian" only appears three times in the New Testament and twice, it is arguably used in a negative sense. "Christian" is a noun. It means "follower of Christ." It cannot be used as an adjective and hope to make any difference in the character, nature, or status of anything it modifies. Listening to Christian music doesn't make you a Christian any more than having a Christian funeral sends you to heaven! Being born in the United States makes you blessed, but it doesn't make you redeemed. If you're unsaved, you can immigrate to America and become an American, but unless you are changed by the power of the Holy Spirit, you're still unsaved. I doubt the previous sentences would be objected to by any Christian on face value, but under the surface and generally unspoken is a definite correlation between citizenship in the United States and citizenship in heaven.

From this un-Biblical correlation comes one major error. It is believed that Jeremiah 29:11 and 2 Chronicles 7:14 speak of America, and more specifically, the one who holds the office of President of the United States. While God loves everyone and wishes *that none should perish but that all should come to repentance*, He doesn't give us extra credit simply because we are Americans. If we are to think Biblically, the exact opposite may be true; those who *know* the truth and reject it are in a much more desperate spiritual condition than those who have never heard the gospel. There can be no doubt that people in our country are more likely to have heard the gospel message than many others in places where freedom is only a far-off, dim dream.

The problem of the political Church is *not* that Christians shouldn't be involved in politics, or that it's *wrong* to be patriotic, but rather that politics and Americanism too often takes precedent over actually following Jesus! The extreme right-wingers have knee jerk negative reactions to compassion ministries while the extreme left-wingers think it's the government's job to enforce the commands of Jesus to feed the hungry, clothe the naked, and heal the sick. Those are all responsibilities that He gave to the Church, not civil authorities.

Had the early church waited until favorable political winds blew, we would have a very short New Testament. Pentecostal power, however, was sufficient to empower and embolden the early disciples to walk forth from their heavenly equipping into a brand-new world where the overcoming power of God proved superior to Roman political might and Jewish religious influence!

The Church has never since ceased to exist, though many have tried to destroy it, and the Church never *will* cease to exist until Christ raptures it from the earth. This Church does not fly a nation's flag or fight with weapons of man; it does not depend on who is in the White House or which party controls the Senate or the House. It is the Church of the living God, with a membership not of earthly citizens but of transformed, redeemed children of God, washed with the blood of the Lamb!

Knowing our human nature and judging from my personal shortcomings, there's clearly something within our physical DNA that often looks for loopholes and shortcuts. If there's an easier way, we'll find it; if there's a way to blame something or someone else for our failures, we'll use it. It's probably the most heeded temptation of our enemy, the devil, and likely because it appeals to our pride. If anyone knows about pride, it's the one who was kicked out of heaven because of it! When we are told what to do, there's a sin-influenced proclivity to question it. When we are faced with our own failure, blaming others is often the first response. This universal human weakness is exacerbated by a fiercely independent spirit like the one you find in the United States of America. Having spoken with pastors in the western United States, the "cowboy" mentality is often the biggest hinderance to getting people saved! The "I can handle life myself" way of thinking does not see the need for Jesus. Until we realize that we are individually responsible to a holy God and desperately unable to live according to His standards, there can be no born-again experience. Why? Because an unrepentant person bases his goodness on his own righteousness and blames his mistakes on his own struggles, often represented by other people.

This same condition exists when politics or nationality is substituted for a living relationship with God. In this case, the loophole to a personal relationship with Jesus Christ is citizenship in a "Christian" country or membership in the "right" political party. The shortcut to facing personal sin is blaming people from the *other* country or *other* party. Aside from the obvious spiritual pitfalls, this also causes blindness to the actions of one's own "camp," refusing to believe that your country or your party could *ever* be guilty of wrongdoing.

Jesus doesn't look upon our political affiliations or earthly citizenship. He isn't concerned with whether our nation is called "Christian" or not. That may not mean much to American Christians, but it is reason for rejoicing for many who live in the 10/40 Window, that area of the world where the majority of countries have made it very difficult for its citizens to follow Jesus! While their earthly future may be bleak, they can have hope in the assurance of their eventual heavenly home. Presently, the fastest growing Church in the world is in Iran. Iran, where it is illegal to be a Christian. What glorious rewards wait for those who, in the face of certain persecution and excommunication from their families, have surrendered every part of themselves to Jesus! Meanwhile, so many in the American political church sing, "I Surrender All," with absolutely *no intention* of doing so, because it just might diminish our personal "rights." God, forgive us.

God's truth is absolute. It's not Republican or Democrat, and it's not American or European. Followers of Jesus should be on the side of truth, regardless of who is proclaiming it. We don't get a pass on what we say, how we react, or what we support just because our "camp" encourages or discourages it. People are people and have the capacity for good or evil. God doesn't excuse sinful behavior in our lives if we consider our actions to be not as bad as the *other* side.

Political polarization, which is at an all-time high, at least in the United States, creates strong division based upon identity. That identity rarely has anything to do with the Kingdom of God. When I was a child, I remember hearing stories about Antichrist, and how he will amass loyalty from many people, convincing them that he is the true messiah. I often wondered how that could be possible. How could one person garner such allegiance? When I step back and examine the current global situation today, it makes perfect sense; someone will come on the scene that will appeal to "both sides," promising a solution that everyone will be happy with. Then, he will turn on everyone. If my eschatology is correct, the true Church won't be here for that, but those who were counting on their political stand to count before God may no doubt be surprised that, as Americans, they were left behind.

What do you think would happen if...the American church got its politics in perspective—being as dedicated to living like Jesus as it is blaming the other camp for what is wrong with society? What do you think would happen if those who confessed Jesus as Savior refused to turn a blind eye to the sin in their *own* camp and determined to live lives of holiness unto the Lord? What if followers of Jesus identified with Jesus *first and foremost*, over and above nation or political party?

CHAPTER SEVEN

...if the Church Got a Handle on Giving?

I don't know about you, but I'm weary of preachers begging for money. I've done it, although I think I convinced myself then that it wasn't really begging. It was simply "presenting the need." The problem is, most people don't *give* to a need, unless that need is accompanied by disturbing images, be it hungry or sick children, or impoverished people on the other side of the globe. Some guy standing there in a $1,000 suit with a dazzling, surgically altered smile is not, however, the kind of image that says "need." In the 1980's, this may have been successful. Those were the days before the public fall of Hollywood-style ministries, when greed and mismanagement could be readily packaged as contemporary versions of Solomon's Temple. Times have (thankfully) changed. No longer does the Church get a pass on exorbitant spending, claiming since the "world" lives well, so should God's servants.

The information age has leveled the playing field, so to speak, when it comes to who knows what about the inner workings of Wall Street, the White House, and indeed, the Church. Leaks are commonplace and authenticity is championed and expected. I sometimes borrow a phrase I heard several years ago from a pastor friend who said while he may not always be able to be transparent, he must always be authentic. Not only is this true in the Church, but it also finds traction in other areas of public life. The politician who in the past could get by with "double talko longer gets a pass on the numerous 24/7 news outlets of the twenty-first century. The financial elites' spending habits are no longer a closely guarded secret, known only to a close circle of like-minded cohorts, and laws that protect the public from unscrupulous religious practices have shed the light of disclosure on the fiscal practices of high-profile ministers and churches.

While some may lament these changes and long for the "good old days" when business could be conducted behind solid doors as opposed to glass, I think it's been good, especially for the Church of Jesus Christ, to be a bit more open and honest about the use of funds which have been solicited for the purpose of spreading the gospel. While it's true that there are times when too much transparency only serves to give snooping eyes a reason to find fault, full disclosure, within reasonable limits, goes a long way in building public confidence, especially in the local church.

I still tire of preachers begging for money. I don't do it anymore. As believers in Christ, we should be the most generous people on earth! God has given us everything! It's fun to give! It's good to give! We should desire to sow good seed into good soil for good reasons to support good causes and ministries. While most Christians say it's important to give to the church, the majority do not tithe, and after all the begging and pleading and sermons and campaigns and programs, not much ever changes. Considering that fact, there's a problem. If we claim to be transformed by the power of the Holy Spirit into new creations, why are there so few who are willing to open their hands unless someone guilts them into doing so?

Maybe we have made too big a distinction between secular and sacred in encouraging generous hearts. God created everyone, whether they choose to follow His Son or not. All people are created in the image of God, even if they never decide to reflect His image in the ideals they cherish and represent. The bottom line is this: people spend their money on what they perceive as valuable. That value may be determined in what brings them pleasure or in what gives them security, or in what makes them feel like they are contributing to society, but the motivation to spend is *usually* related to the value of the item being exchanged for cash. I say *usually* because there is an exception to this rule. The exception is guilt! I don't know about you, but I don't appreciate that tactic, whether it is being employed by a preacher or a used-car salesman! How can we tell people that the Holy Spirit regenerates hearts one minute and attempt to manipulate hearts the next?

Radical generosity is one thing the world's system can't counterfeit. It might even be an annoying source of envy for the unscrupulous who seek to paint Christian leaders as money-hungry and self-aggrandizing. I sure hope so! I've heard it said and have personally adopted the philosophy that an effective leader never asks his potential followers to do anything he's not willing to do himself. What do you think would happen in the Church Universal if leaders led the way in radical generosity? What would happen in the local church if the pastors were the first to step up to demonstrate liberal giving? What if professing Christians in a community researched ways to be generous, both in time and money, to things that glorify God and benefit the marginalized in society?

If what we do and what we choose *not* to do is based upon the condition of our hearts, how can we separate generosity from the more obvious indicators of holy living? How can we expect to live overtly sanctified lives and be embarrassingly stingy at the same time? Talk is cheap and emotions are fickle. Extravagant giving isn't restricted to Sunday morning when the offering plate makes its rounds. If we allow God to give us generous hearts, that will spill over to the people we meet daily.

> James 2:15-16 NLT reads, "Suppose you see a brother or sister who has no food or clothing, and you say, 'Good-bye and have a good day; stay warm and eat well'—but then you don't give that person any food or clothing. What good does that do?"

Note this admonition is directed to a "brother or sister;" the Greek here is *Adelphos* for brother and *Adelphe* for sister. While this can be used to denote literal family, it is most often used in New Testament scripture to indicate fellow Christians. Are we willing to give to fellow believers who are facing difficult times without expecting anything in return? How many times?

I realize this is a sensitive topic, and I understand the questions: "How many times is too many?" "At what point does mercy become enablement?" Believe me, I get it. I've been there too! Perhaps there is another question that would best be asked alongside: "Is giving to alleviate need only expressed in dollars and cents?" Could giving to the less fortunate also take the form of helping them make better decisions, or helping them learn a skill? This takes *more* than just money; it takes an investment of time. Genuine revival in the heart of a believer not only yields extravagant giving in terms of finances, but of time as well. I would argue that time is even *more* difficult to surrender without expecting something back, but wouldn't this type of giving, in most cases, make a bigger impact?

How many times have you heard someone say, "You can only do so much"? I hear it quite often, especially from other believers who have become weary of being taken for granted in the area of doing for others. While it's true that we can "only do so much," we rarely do! It takes a level of patience and empathy that can only come from the Holy Spirit, and even then, we can get weary. The problem arises when we try to understand the poor choices of others based upon our own good stewardship habits. This is an exercise in futility, and it will leave us frustrated! After all, if those who continually seem to operate in crisis mode had better time and money management skills, they wouldn't need to ask for help so often. How can we best help people who always seem to be asking? In many cases, the answer is not throwing money at the problem, but instead, investing our time, talents, and experience with them.

In regards to giving to non-believers in crisis, there is great opportunity for witness on the part of the Christian in demonstrating the love, mercy, and grace of God. Some have been condemned by "church people" in the past and need to see the *real deal* in action. Look at the way Jesus blessed the crowds who were following Him, many of which had been dismissed by the religious crowd. Jesus never excused sin, but He was always loving to sinners. What do you think would happen if the unbelieving world saw sacrificial giving on the part of those who claim to follow Jesus, and they had to really dig to find it? You know, that whole "don't let your left hand know what your right hand does" principle that Jesus commanded in Matthew's gospel. What impact could be made for the Kingdom of God were we to practice radical generosity and did it in such a way that no one knew about it? This will set you free, and it can only be done through the indwelling, empowering Holy Spirit. It's just not *natural* for people to be anonymously magnanimous—it's *super*-natural!

Generosity cannot be mandated; it must be internalized. Jesus was more generous than any of us could ever be. After all, He was God in the flesh, but set all that aside to be a servant, even to the point of death on a cross. If we've been changed by the Holy Spirit into new creatures, giving should be a way of life! We should *look* for ways to give out of a thankful heart that's overflowing in love, compassion, and empathy. The very fact that some believers are so stingy with their time, talents, and resources is very troubling to me. If we've been born again, shouldn't that new life be one of radical hospitality? What do you think would happen if people who claim to follow Jesus would follow His example of selflessness in front of a critical, yet hurting world? Don't you think it would begin to change how the unbelieving crowd views Christians? How could it not?

Have you ever thought about how much fun it would be to have a million dollars to give away? You'd see a worthy cause or a dire need and for once, you would have the means to make a real difference! Perhaps lack of finances is not an issue for you, but your time is; the commitments in your life leave little time for you to give away. What if time was on your side? What would you do for others, where would you invest your talents, gifts, and attention—if time wasn't an issue? Maybe your health situation restricts your physical movement, but you dream about being able to use your hands and feet to meet critical needs.

May I suggest that the same joy you are imagining right now could become reality by adjusting priorities in proportion to what you *do* have available, and setting out to make the most of the resources you have? What do you think would happen if Christ followers put the words of Jesus into practical application,

> *"give, and it will be given to you. Good measure, pressed down, shaken together, running over, will be put into your lap. For with the measure you use it will be measured back to you."*
>
> *(Luke 6:38 ESV)*

This doesn't mean your finances. In context, Jesus wasn't talking about finances at all, but of forgiving others! Church, we need to hear this today in a time where so many live in a perpetual state of offence! When we loosen our grip on our money, our time, our service, and yes, even our offense, God will release blessing into our lives in abundance—above anything we could possibly imagine.

At our church, we established a vision team to seek God about some short and long-term goals and a fresh vision statement and core values that reflect not only where we are now, but where we want to be. One of our core values is, "Extravagant Generosity." We defined that as being "Spirit-led stewards of God's gifts to do His work." This means more than finances, but includes *all* kingdom investments, be that monetary or otherwise. There is a conviction that we are here for a reason, and that is to introduce people to and help them follow Jesus! In a self-centered world, this kind of extravagance gets noticed. Some will mock the devoted disciple for being fanatical, but others, who have beer by religious church people, are attracted to the gen

What today's culture defines as radical giving isn' at all. It's Biblical! Christ gave His all for us. Ho consider giving Him our second best in return? What do you thi would happen if extravagant generosity became the norm in our churches? Just imagine a team comprised of "professional" and lay ministers, working side by side, pulling together with kingdom goals to reach the world! Call me a dreamer, but I envision this in our current divided and cynical society. When this present shaking is in our rear-view mirror, when government programs and plans have failed, and when the economy has collapsed and our once great nation no longer looks the same, what will the Church look like? My prayer is that the remnant will be leading the way. My hope is that the Church—the true bride of Christ—will have found her way, that a Holy Spirit-empowered, lean, forward moving machine will lead the world into preparation for the great and glorious return of our King, "*to present her to himself as a radiant church, without stain or wrinkle or any other blemish, but holy and blameless.*" *(Ephesians 5:27 NIV)*

CHAPTER EIGHT

...if We Embraced God's Creativity?

Then Moses said to the people of Israel,

> "See, the Lord has called by name Bezalel the son of Uri, son of Hur, of the tribe of Judah; and he has filled him with the Spirit of God, with skill, with intelligence, with knowledge, and with all craftsmanship, to devise artistic designs, to work in gold and silver and bronze, in cutting stones for setting, and in carving wood, for work in every skilled craft. And he has inspired him to teach, both him and Oholiab the son of Ahisamach of the tribe of Dan. He has filled them with skill to do every sort of work done by an engraver or by a designer or by an embroiderer in blue and purple and scarlet yarns and fine twined linen, or by a weaver—by any sort of workman or skilled designer.
>
> (Exodus 35:30-35 ESV)

I've enjoyed watching home improvement shows, where over the course of half an hour, a house is transformed from a sad looking fixer-upper to the pride of the neighborhood. Some people watch these shows and opt to adopt an orphan house of their own, inspired by the professionals on these television shows who make it all look so easy. Many are quick to find out that the work and struggle in between "cuts" on their favorite TV show to be more than they bargained for, and they either give up before the transformation is complete or end up sinking way too much money into the venture.

Not everyone is skilled enough to restore an old, run-down house or to accurately count the cost before undertaking a major project. But God, in His creative office, has uniquely and wonderfully created human beings to be, in His image, creative. We are all different; that may be His greatest creative achievement! Of all the people on Planet Earth at any given time, none are exactly alike. Some are short, some are tall; some are skinny, some are gravitationally enhanced! All are creative—in some way—believer or non-believer, simply because *all* are creations of God.

When the Holy Spirit regenerates a heart, however, and another soul is made clean, the capacity to create increases exponentially. Why? Because God Himself, in the person of the Holy Spirit, is now able to reside on the inside, because that *creation* of God has now become a *child* of God! The child always bears a similarity to his father, and as born-again followers of Jesus, we are re-made to look like our Heavenly Father. A big part of that likeness is creativity. The Church, through the centuries, has embraced and sponsored this truth. Much of the classical music that history regards as the finest of all time was commissioned by the Church. Some of the greatest art, the ceiling of the Sistine Chapel for instance, would not exist without the initiative and sponsorship of the Church. Christian literature, such as Bunyan's *Pilgrim's Progress* and Milton's *Paradise Lost,* is valued for its stylistic contribution, as well as its religious content. The same God inspired all these creative works, and the Church is often the producer and first recipient.

The Church has also been highly effective at problem solving through God-given creativity. Most of the first institutions of higher learning were established by the Church. The first hospitals, clinics, adoption agencies, and other community aid organizations were, in great part, brought into existence by the Church. Whenever a new and efficient way of meeting a societal need came into being, its impetus was, in many cases, the Church. God-inspired compassion plus the power of the Holy Spirit equals a divine solution!

Consider the first problem that came up in the early Church that we read about in Acts Chapter 6; the Greek-speaking widows were going hungry because of a language and culture barrier. The solution? The Church appointed seven men who were full of the Holy Spirit and wisdom to ensure that these women would not be overlooked. Now, it may not seem unusual to us to appoint a committee to handle this issue, but remember, the Church was brand new! For the Jewish follower of Jesus living in first-century Israel, this had never happened before. Now that faith in Christ was the identifier over nationality and a common language, new problems were arising that needed to be met with God's creativity.

In the passage of scripture from Exodus 35 at the beginning of this chapter, God was downloading a whole lot of information to Moses about the construction of the tent of meeting. It was the Tabernacle and would be built in the wilderness of Sinai. Moses was the perfect example of an unwilling leader. He didn't feel worthy of the task, but he listened to God and took on the enormous job of leading rebellious Israel toward the promised land. It seems history looks fondly upon people who were hesitant to accept the mantle of leadership. Perhaps humility is a far greater strength than many of the leadership assessment tests would indicate.

While Moses' duties were many, God didn't plan for him to do everything on his own. In the case of the Tabernacle, God gave Moses the blueprints, but He gave others the skills to complete the work. In the passage above, Moses tells the people that God,

> has filled [Bezalel] with the Spirit of God, with skill, with intelligence, with knowledge, and with all craftsmanship, to devise artistic designs, to work in gold and silver and bronze, in cutting stones for setting, and in carving wood, for work in every skilled craft.
>
> (Exodus 35:31-33 ESV)

This is, arguably, the first instance of someone being filled with the Spirit of God in the Bible, and what was the result? Bezalel was given the ability to work artistically in precious metals and stones and in the carving of wood! Can you see a contemporary spiritual gifts survey containing these skills? Creativity is important to God, because in this fallen world, He knows we will need Divine inspiration and equipping to not only navigate ourselves, but to help others along the way.

How many people sit in church pews week after week thinking they have nothing to offer the Kingdom of God because they see no outlet for their giftings? Perhaps, they aren't even *aware* of their giftings. Although they have value, after all the spiritual gift surveys have been completed and all the discipleship books have been written, the fact is we are simply *made* to be and do what God has *created* us to be and do. Granted, that often takes some time to figure out, but God-given passion fuels God-given mission! Where we are creatively fulfilled is likely a good place to start serving and ministering! While education is extremely important, you can't get a college degree in creativity and passion. What do you think would happen if children of God found an outlet for their God-given creativity in a way that blessed others and contributed to the Kingdom of God, instead of seeking positions, opportunities, and spiritual gifts from a perspective of what is *expected* of them by others?

Having some background in the building trades, I very much enjoy getting out from behind my desk every so often and getting my hands dirty with a building project for the church or helping in a benevolence project. Building and rebuilding is a big part of who I am, and without this creative outlet, I wouldn't feel like I was truly contributing where I'm gifted. Music is another huge part of my life. Arranging vocals and singing is something that has been integral to my very soul for longer than I can even remember. To *not* offer these gifts creatively for the Glory of God would be denying part of what God designed me to be! If I was told that music and working with my hands was not a viable means of service in the Kingdom of God, I would be *crushed*! I would not be complete as a minister. The truth is, the same Holy Spirit that enables me to write, preach, and lead a church also enables me to sing, arrange music, pull wire, and finish drywall!

In the past couple of decades, creativity in ministry has been rightfully pushed to the front of the line, and that's a *good* thing! Whenever I see a new church setting up in a shopping mall or another public marketplace, I get excited! When I hear of daring young ministers being used by God in non-traditional ways, outside of a physical church location, my heart beats just a little faster. Compassion ministries that set out to bless the marginalized of society by going to them, bringing hope where only despair had been, are like a soothing balm to weary souls. There are those trapped in self-replicating cycles of poverty and abuse that don't know that there is freedom in Christ! There are people existing multi-generationally in financial debt simply because they don't have money management skills, and no one has ever been able to intervene. Most of these people won't come to church, but they need creative, Spirit-filled leaders to come alongside them and break the chains of defeat that they wear and inevitably pass along to their children. I applaud the contemporary ministers and ministries that are allowing the Holy Spirit to equip them to serve these non-brick-and-mortar parishes.

If we really think about it, this is a picture of the restored New Testament Church. Most of what has historically been considered *essentials* of church planting and church growth are out the window today, and I, for one, am glad to see it! Don't get me wrong, I love Sunday mornings at 10 a.m. and look forward to the time of corporate worship each week, but it can't end there. I firmly believe, in our post-COVID world, that the Church will be forever changed for the better! The seasons of lock-down we have experienced have caused the dreamers to flourish, while those stuck in the dry valley of tradition and human effort are floundering. I take no pleasure in seeing churches close, but if that means that the brakes are off to what God wants to do, so be it.

In 1999, Rev. Verlon Fosner assumed the pastorate of a 90-year-old Assemblies of God congregation in Seattle, Washington. To say that pastoring a church in the Pacific Northwest is challenging is an understatement. Religious affiliation is markedly lower than the national average, resulting in a majority secular society. Fosner recognized that the old way of doing things wasn't working, though the need to reach those identifying as "nones" (those with no religious affiliation) was increasing. In 2004, with the realization that the decline in attendance at the church was unsustainable over the long run, the leadership planted a different kind of church in a nearby urban neighborhood. They called it "Agape Feast Church." The format was based upon the early New Testament Church—around the dinner table!

The results were mind-blowing! Every week, hundreds of "nones" gathered to share a meal together and talk about Jesus! Soon, the movement multiplied into many more such churches in other areas, and eventually expanded into a national network. People who would likely have never entered the doors of a traditional church were coming to faith in Christ because Christians cared enough to bring Jesus to them! Eventually, the traditional proclamation model, called Westminster Community Church, became Community Dinners Fellowship. The existing church building was leased out to another congregation, helping to fund this new ministry model. The organizers of what became known as The Dinner Church Collective discovered an interesting reality: seculars weren't opposed to Jesus as much as they were His representatives! When the walls of religion were removed, the real Jesus was revealed![8]

Not every traditional church has to be replaced as was the case in Seattle, Washington, but what do you think would happen if God's Church got the green light from its leaders to passionately pursue its God-given creativity, even if that meant it would never look the same again? Is it indeed possible to move beyond pews and a steeple to the point that Joe Average would have his opinion of "Church People" changed forever? Are we, the Church, willing to let God's Spirit do what He wants to do and become a mobilized, unified force in the world, truly making disciples for Jesus—even if our sacred Sunday morning traditions must change? It's hard to change, but if we don't change, we die. The good news is, God has enough creativity in His proverbial little finger to transform the world, through us, if we will just let Him!

We live in an age of shaking—politically, socially, religiously—and we can become weary of how quickly our long-treasured foundations are shifting and becoming more unstable. As followers of Jesus, we must remember that we have been warned about this. Hebrews 12:28-29 reminds us of our precious identity in Christ like this:

> *Therefore let us be grateful for receiving a kingdom that cannot be shaken, and thus let us offer to God acceptable worship, with reverence and awe, for our God is a consuming fire. (ESV)*

When everything temporal is shaken to its core, remember, child of God, your citizenship is not in this word's kingdom, but in God's! Live in gratitude for the heavenly Kingdom you *are receiving.* We don't just hang on until Heaven; our Kingdom experience begins at the moment of salvation and continues for eternity! Since we are part of the Creator's Kingdom, let's not become beaten down along with those who have no hope, but continue to be creative in how we reach the lost with the good news of Jesus Christ! *What do you think would happen if* the Church employed creative faith in terms of how we make disciples, while continuing to handle the glorious unchanging gospel Biblically, honestly, and authentically?

CHAPTER NINE

...if We Made Ourselves of No Reputation?

> Let this mind be in you which was also in Christ Jesus, who, being in the form of God, did not consider it robbery to be equal with God, but made Himself of no reputation, taking the form of a bondservant, and coming in the likeness of men.
>
> (Philippians 2:5-7 NKJV)

Which is better, to be humble or to *be* humbled? I'm sure we've all experienced the latter, and wished we'd have adopted the former instead! Humility goes a long way in being unified when it comes to relationships in families, society, and the Church. Jesus set the bar high in this area as the scripture passage from Philippians 2 elaborates so succinctly. Jesus not only "made Himself of no reputation," He went even further; He became a servant, a bondservant, by definition: One who surrenders his own interests for the sake of others. His very nature as God in the flesh adds to the magnitude of His willingness to assume this position.

While the language of Philippians 2:7 in the New King James Version (above) contains the phrase "*made Himself of no reputation,*" I don't believe it is the most faithful way to translate the intent of this verse, although it does make for a provocative chapter title. The word which is translated as the phrase "no reputation" is the Greek *kenoo.* It means *to make empty* or *void.* The English Standard Version does a good job of rendering verses 5-7 as follows:

> Have this mind among yourselves, which is yours in Christ Jesus, who, though he was in the form of God, did not

> count equality with God a thing to be grasped, but emptied himself, by taking the form of a servant, being born in the likeness of men.

The emphasis is striking. Jesus emptied Himself—He made Himself of no reputation—by becoming a servant, surrendering His own interests for the sake of others, and becoming one of us! A human being! Born into this world in much the same manner as the ones He came to save, except for that whole born-of-a-virgin thing, of course. Have you ever really contemplated the humiliation of the incarnation==that the Creator became a creation for the *sake* of His creation? The ESV more correctly translates verse 6 as well, stating that Jesus, while equal with God, did not pursue His rightful position; He didn't take it by force, as a robber would, but surrendered it for you and for me.

I don't remember who it was, but a pastor once told me that upon his ordination, an older minister told him to protect his reputation at all costs. He related how that struck him, considering the scripture passage from Philippians 2. He wondered how he could place so great an emphasis on protecting what other people thought of him when Jesus so freely dismissed it! My mother, a preacher's kid, used to tell me how, when she was a teenager, my grandmother would always remind her to "remember who your father is," when she was leaving the house to enjoy activities with her friends. She told me she resented it, because she had never given my grandparents any trouble, any reason to doubt her public morality. Only as she got older did she understand the pious nature of some church people who are just looking for anything to be critical about.

Had Jesus been concerned about His reputation, He wouldn't have opened His mouth in the presence of the Jewish religious leaders, not to mention challenge them! If Jesus was concerned about receiving the credit due Him, He would have never become the Son of man, who came to seek and save the lost! In the same way, if our reputation—what others think of us—is the most closely guarded aspect of who we are, we can't possibly be like Jesus! In what ways do we do this, and how can we change? Perhaps it would be good to consider what we might want to empty ourselves of.

Our Rights

The Declaration of Independence asserts:

> We hold these truths to be self-evident, that all men are created equal, that they are endowed by their Creator with certain unalienable rights, that among these are Life, Liberty, and the pursuit of Happiness.

Unalienable means they cannot be taken away by any person or government; these rights come directly from God. This is a precious value that is worth defending! It is foundational to freedom as we define it in the United States of America. When we expand personal rights beyond that which the Word of God grants us, however, we run the risk of being in opposition to the heart and mind of Christ. Our current societal climate is replete with voices clamoring for "their rights" in the most minute categories imaginable. A substantial percentage of the population takes personal offense at so much, even to the point of seemingly inventing new things to be offended by every day!

There is no one who has surrendered more personal rights than Jesus. He didn't do it out of intimidation or a poor self-image; He did it willingly for people who needed a spiritual heart transplant, and He is calling us to do the same. If one claims no allegiance to the Kingdom of God, they are free to be as self-centered as they choose, but for the child of God, a different standard is to be realized. The Church should be a bastion of selfless humility, leading the charge in laying down personal rights for the sake of others! What do you think would happen if believers in and followers of Jesus Christ followed His example in placing others' rights ahead of our own?

Our Desire for Credit

The Jewish religious leaders were often the object of Jesus' sermons, particularly when their outward displays of righteousness contrasted with their inner self-centeredness. As Jesus gave the admonition to His hearers on the mountainside regarding giving to the needy, He said that it is better to give to those in need and remain anonymous than to give publicly that others may see. To emphasize the point, He said, "But when you give to someone in need, don't let your left hand know what your right hand is doing." (Matthew 6:3, NLT)

Of course, it's physically impossible to achieve this, but the implication is clear. If you're giving just to receive credit for giving, that's all the reward you will ever get. However, if you give in anonymity, refusing to even acknowledge the act to yourself, God will reward you for it. I'm sure this was a hard teaching for Jesus' first audience, being surrounded by the ceremony- loving Pharisees who loved to draw public attention to their pious acts of charity. It may be just as difficult for us today. I believe, however, we can take it even one step further.

Apply this to our need to be noticed, to receive our due credit, to be recognized for our achievements, specifically in the Church. What if we were to lay aside the desire to attach our name to an especially good idea? What if we were okay with someone else getting the credit for a successful community program or outreach? Would it be acceptable for the congregation, as a single entity, to be credited for its positive achievements without attaching any single person's name to them?

Here's another way to look at the issue of credit. First, if a local church reaches out to their community to present the gospel to those who are far from God and people come to know the Lord as a result, is the outreach still a success if those who were saved begin attending another church, rather than the one who sponsored the outreach? Secondly, if a church plants a new church in a neighboring town, but the new church plant grows faster than the sending church, is there as much celebrating on the part of the parent church as there would have been if it were still the larger congregation? The answer to both questions *must* be a resounding "Yes!" Why? Because the goal is Kingdom growth. If that isn't the answer, and the goal *isn't* Kingdom growth but instead earthly reputation, it would have been more honest to just admit that from the beginning.

Colossians 3:1 says, "Since, then, you have been raised with Christ, set your hearts on things above, where Christ is, seated at the right hand of God." (NIV) This speaks to having a heavenly perspective in all we do. Verse 5 of the same chapter reads, "Put to death, therefore, whatever belongs to your earthly nature: sexual immorality, impurity, lust, evil desires and greed, which is idolatry." (NIV) Under the category of *impurity*, can we not add earthly motivations such as the desire for credit and recognition? Funny how certain of the list in verse 5 make it into sermon outlines while others do not.

What do you think would happen if Christians did what was right, and did it often, without the need of recognition for doing so? What might be the outcome of doing something outrageously generous for someone else and working outrageously hard to remain anonymous? What if different local churches found ways to work together so that only God received the credit for what was accomplished? Naïve? No! Biblical? I think so! The world is watching. Unbelievers have seen the ugliness of jealousy and greed within the organized church and will notice the difference that selflessness makes. You say you want to reach the lost? Great! Then let's live like the found! What do you think would happen? What do we have to lose, except our reputation?

PART B:
BE THE CHURCH

CHAPTER TEN

The Church at Ephesus

> John, To the seven churches in the province of Asia: Grace and peace to you from him who is, and who was, and who is to come, and from the seven spirits before his throne, and from Jesus Christ, who is the faithful witness, the firstborn from the dead, and the ruler of the kings of the earth. To him who loves us and has freed us from our sins by his blood, and has made us to be a kingdom and priests to serve his God and Father—to him be glory and power for ever and ever! Amen.
>
> (Revelation 1:4-6 NIV)

If you ask the question about what it means to be the Church, you'll get as many answers as there are Christian denominations; reportedly, that would be about 41,000! Why are there so many different opinions on exactly what the Church is and what its people should be doing? I suppose because it's difficult to cross cultural, linguistic, and geographical divides to come up with a distilled answer that all would agree on. Perhaps the best we can do is answer the question in our own context.

Each local gathering of believers has its own personality, gifts, calling, and purpose. A good example of this is found in the book of Revelation, the letter to the seven churches in Asia, chapters 2 and 3. This is the letter that the risen and ascended Jesus dictated through the apostle John on the island of Patmos. In most instances, Jesus had some good things to say about these churches as well as some not-so-good things to say. It's a healthy and productive exercise to ask ourselves in the twenty-first century,

"What would Jesus have to say about *our* church?" and then act upon His answer. In other words, *be the Church!*

Sound good? Let's do it! Let's look at each representation of the Body of Christ in the seven cities to whom Jesus has John write. At the least, we will receive a blessing from God (read Revelation 1:3); at the most, we'll hear from God on what "being the Church" looks like. Be ready, also, to discover what "being the Church" *doesn't* look like. Some of life's greatest lessons are indeed these. Each church mentioned in this letter existed at the time John received this heavenly dictation, each experiencing its own unique set of problems and virtues. The Church throughout history has also exhibited these characteristics and descriptions. The Church today, no doubt, can be found in the pages of this revelation of God to man. One common feature of all these churches is a promise Jesus made to those who "would endure to the end." That's a promise to overcomers! We can take great comfort today in the fact that all God's promises are "yes," and "amen!" (2 Corinthians 1:20) The greatest blessing we can receive from a study of Revelation 2 and 3 is to know that no matter what we encounter as we walk forward in faith, we are designed to live as overcomers in a fallen world!

Ephesus – Revelation 2:1-7

At the time of the writing of Revelation, Ephesus was a major coastal city in the Roman Empire. Today, due to years of silt buildup, it sits several miles inland in southwestern Turkey. The church in Ephesus, in the late first century, was a large, powerful church having a collection of congregations, perhaps hundreds! The culture of the day was a religious mixture with a large concentration of pagan and magic arts. One major feature of Ephesus was the presence of the temple of the Roman goddess Diana (Artemis), one of the Seven Wonders of the Ancient World. The chief cult of Ephesus was Artemis.

Founded during the Apostle Paul's Third Missionary Journey in the mid-fifties AD, this church was a mature, growing congregation. It had the benefit of some famous spiritual leaders among its inhabitants. For example, Timothy, the ministerial son of Paul, was a pastoral leader here, and the Apostle John lived and ministered here until his death near the close of the first century. It was from Ephesus that John wrote the Gospel of John and the three Epistles of John. It was on nearby Patmos that John had the vision contained herein. Ephesus was a powerful city; the church in Ephesus was a powerful church. However, Jesus had some things against them and had warnings for them.

The Church in Ephesus was doctrinally sound, consisted of hard workers performing good deeds with perseverance, and it had no time for false teachers and false apostles—those who claimed to have known Christ, but also claimed authority they did not have. They endured hardships for the name of Christ and did not grow weary. Man, this church had it going on! They were hard workers and sticklers for good doctrine! All these attributes are good, and the members of this thriving church were to be commended for not taking their hands off the plow! However, there was a problem; they had lost their love. Their *first* love. The love of God, of each other, and of the lost.

Doctrine is important, but we can't worship doctrine. Worship is important, but we can't worship worship. A good reputation, strong work ethic, purity, and perseverance are all good qualities of a church, but if initiated without love, what good is it? Mahatma Gandhi said, "I like your Christ, but don't care for Christians." God help us if this is true of us today, and I fear in some instances it is. The liberals talk about loving one another, and the fundamentalists hear "license to sin!" The fundamentalists talk about the importance of sound doctrine, and the liberals hear "lack of grace!" Standing firm on Biblical doctrine and loving like Jesus are not mutually exclusive! It's not one or the other, it's both! Strong doctrine + first love = a healthy church! Jesus brought this sin of lovelessness to the forefront for the Ephesian church of the first century, and He sheds His holy light on the twenty-first century church today.

> Consider how far you have fallen! Repent and do the things you did at first. If you do not repent, I will come to you and remove your lampstand from its place.
>
> (Revelation 2:5 NIV)

God doesn't usually remove our memories. The bad ones encourage us not to repeat the failures of the past while the good ones help us evaluate the present. This helps us remember how we started with Christ to see if we've fallen from the ideal, and if so, how far. His Holy Spirit gives us warnings to repent and the consequences if we don't. The Church in Ephesus was a prominent church in a prominent city. Even during social depravity, the church was, by all external metrics, thriving, but they had forgotten what motivated them in the first place—love. Thankfully, Jesus gave a promise to those who would make the needed corrections in Ephesus:

> Whoever has ears, let them hear what the Spirit says to the churches. To the one who is victorious, I will give the right to eat from the tree of life, which is in the paradise of God.
>
> (Revelation 2:7 NIV)

Can we relate to the church in Ephesus? Are we surrounded by pagan influence? Can we thrive in spite of it? What positive characteristics of the first century Ephesian church do you see in your church today? What negatives? What can you do to make a difference? What do you think would happen if you did?

CHAPTER ELEVEN

The Church at Smyrna – Revelation 2:8-11

While Ephesus was home to the goddess Artemis, Smyrna was home to the god Dionysus, of whom it was said, "he who became dead and lived." It is fitting, then, that Jesus, through John, greets the church in Smyrna as He did:

> To the angel of the church in Smyrna write: These are the words of him who is the First and the Last, who died and came to life again.
>
> (Revelation 2:8 NIV)

Smyrna was marked with a stark contrast between the very poor and the very rich. The city had a history of "courting Rome," so at this point in history when pagan worship was in revival, there naturally wouldn't have been too much fondness for Christians. Roman law didn't allow new religions, and it only tolerated Judaism. Christianity was initially considered a sect of Judaism. As it became at odds with Judaism from a Roman perspective, the emperor Domitian declared it illegal to be Christian, preferring rather, that worship be directed toward him in a period when the Imperial Cult, or worship of emperors, was gaining momentum.

Polycarp, a disciple of the Apostle John and the first Bishop of Smyrna, was killed for the sake of the Gospel in this city about 60 years after this letter was written. As he was about to be burned at the stake for his testimony of Christ, he was given the chance to recant his faith and save his life. Polycarp is recorded as saying, "I have served Him for eighty-six years, and He has never done me any wrong. Why then should I blaspheme against my King and my Savior?"

The church in Smyrna was poor—poverty stricken, actually—because of the Christian's low place in society. However, it was rich in faithfulness, earning it the title "The Rich Poor Church." Jesus assured the members of the church in Smyrna that He knew what they were up against; He knew about those of "the Synagogue of Satan," obviously religious imposters who had infiltrated their ranks, causing suffering and strife in their antagonism toward the cross of Christ. Jesus told them the persecution was far from over, but that it would have a definite end. He had no condemnation for the believers in Smyrna, only commendation. The Lord concluded His message to this faithful church with a promise:

> Whoever has ears, let them hear what the Spirit says to the churches. The onewho is victorious will not be hurt at all by the second death.
>
> (Revelation 2:11 NIV)

The lesson of the church in Smyrna is that suffering can occur in faith, but fear doesn't have to! James, the half-brother of Jesus, wrote to Jewish Christians living in many different areas of the world:

> Dear brothers and sisters, when troubles of any kind come your way, consider it an opportunity for great joy.
>
> (James 1:2 NLT)

Though suffering is never something we look forward to, it doesn't have to define or defeat us! The Eastern Church understands this better than the Western Church, where most have never experienced the persecution that following Jesus brings to many. In large parts of the Arab world, following Jesus means ostracization by family, friends, and society, much the same way that the believers in Smyrna experienced it. In some cultures, particularly among Muslim fundamentalists, a decision to follow Jesus is almost certainly met with death. When it comes right down to it, however, death cannot destroy a believer in Jesus. It simply changes him from one state of being to another, more perfect, and eternal one!

Can the Church today learn something from Jesus' commendation to the church in Smyrna? What do you think would happen if followers of Jesus stopped seeing suffering as steps to salvation or indictments of personal guilt and simply accepted that not everything is going to be smooth sailing upon a sincere confession of Christ as Savior? Is it possible to embrace suffering for the sake of Christ yet live overcoming, abundant, and joy-filled lives? Of *course,* it is; this is the heart of the gospel!

"Come to Jesus and everything will get easier" is a too-often held belief by some who have been duped either by their own misguided understandings or by the actions of silver-tongued purveyors of easy-believism. Discipleship is costly—it costs you all the world has to offer—but nothing else offers a better return, both in this life and the next. What kind of impact do you suppose the contemporary Church could have if its members truly decided to follow Jesus and never turn back?

CHAPTER TWELVE

The Church at Pergamum (Pergamos) – Revelation 2:12-17

If you were looking for a city in ancient Asia Minor that touted the greatest degradation and godless activity, you would have needed to look no further than Pergamum. During the reign of Domitian, Pergamum was the chief city of emperor worship in the region. Located there were multiple temples of pagan worship, one of them dedicated specifically to Caesar Augustus. The city boasted a large library, second only to the one in Alexandria, Egypt. Jesus described this city in Revelation 2:13 as the city, "*where Satan has his throne,*" and yet He commended this church for remaining *"true to my name."* Any city where Satan is pleased by the lifestyles of the majority of its inhabitants would be a tough place to start a church; however, this church was thriving, and Jesus honored them for remaining true.

Jesus did have some correction for this church, though. Some in the church were acting like Balaam, an interesting character whose story is found in Numbers 22-25. In a nutshell, Balaam pointed out the weakness of Israel to Balak, the King of Moab. Moab was taking part in pagan worship, the very thing God had repeatedly warned them against. Apparently, there were those in the church in Pergamum who were convincing people to take part in the pagan worship that was so prevalent in the city. Others in the church were swayed by the Nicolaitans and their practice of Antinomianism, a belief that Christians did not have to observe moral laws. The church in Ephesus was commended for avoiding this sin; the church in Pergamum had practitioners in its midst, and they were living out this pluralistic doctrine and leading others astray. Verse 16 reads, "Repent therefore! Otherwise, I will soon come to you and will fight against them with the sword of my mouth."

Here, Jesus says He will fight against those who hold to the teaching of Balaam and the Nicolaitans with the sword of His mouth—the sharp, double edged sword that Jesus referenced in His opening words to this church in verse 12. Ephesians 6 refers to the Word as the sword of the Spirit. Jesus promises swift punishment unless these offenders repent. With repentance, however, comes a promise!

> Whoever has ears, let them hear what the Spirit says to the churches. To the one who is victorious, I will give some of the hidden manna. I will also give that person a white stone with a new name written on it, known only to the one who receives it.
>
> (Revelation 2:17 NIV)

The rewards for faithfulness include hidden manna, a sustenance that the pagan people of Pergamum couldn't understand, and a white stone, a not guilty verdict for those who have been made right before God with a new name, meaningful only to the one who receives it. Just like the hidden manna, this new name is one that only makes sense to the overcomer—the faithful and victorious servant of Christ!

Don't we, at times, feel like we don't belong in this world—that we are misunderstood by those "on the outside?" Are we not maligned, at times, for holding eternal treasures more closely than temporal ones? Does it seem like all around us, people are looking everywhere but to God for satisfaction, only to be left empty and unfulfilled? Do they deride you for choosing to live holy and consecrated lives and make fun of your choices? Don't be anxious about being misunderstood, criticized, and mischaracterized, for we share a promise with the believers of the church at Pergamum; if we refuse to deny Jesus and live lives that honor

Him, God has reserved for us righteous vindication far beyond anything this unbelieving world can give.

The bottom line is this: Serving Jesus has eternal benefits! What do you think would happen if the Church adopted vision and mission in keeping with this truth? Would you live your life differently if your goals were not affected by what others think about you? What would your future plans look like? How would you spend your time and money if your only purpose was to live for the approval of God alone? Is there any reason to believe that Jesus has changed His mind about what He told the Church in Pergamum? Has 2,000 years changed His opinion about staying true and not denying His name? Of course, the answer is "No." As the Apostle Paul wrote to the Philippian Church:

> I press toward the goal for the prize of the upward call of God in Christ Jesus.
>
> (Philippians 3:14 NKJV)

CHAPTER THIRTEEN

The Church at Thyatira – Revelation 2:18-29

Thyatira was a small but thriving center of commerce located near the present-day city of

Ak-Hissar, Turkey. It was known for its high concentration of trades and the trade unions that represented them. If you were a tradesman, Thyatira was a "closed shop," which means that you were blackballed if you weren't part of organized labor. The chief deity in town was Apollo, the sun god, and there were many temple feasts and festivities in which the townspeople participated. They included the local tentmakers, sellers of fabric, carpenters, and all the members of their respective unions. If you wanted to earn a living, you needed to join the union. If you wanted to remain in good standing with your union, you went to the parties at the pagan temple.

It's pretty easy to see how this could lead to compromise for the followers of Jesus in Thyatira! Their decision to live holy could literally cause them to starve to death, but Jesus commends them for their faithfulness. "I know your deeds, your love and faith, your service and perseverance, and that you are now doing more than you did at first." (Revelation 2:19 NIV)

Not only are they surviving, they are thriving in love, faith, service, and perseverance! No doubt the members of this church depended heavily on one another for all things—even their very subsistence. There was one troubling compromise, however, that the Lord took them to task for; it was the fact that they tolerated *Jezebel* in their midst. This *Jezebel* was likely not a literal woman named Jezebel, but the spirit of Jezebel, the wife of King Ahab of

Israel. The first mention of this dangerous woman can be found in 1 Kings 16:31, where God considers Ahab's marriage to her a sin, since she was the daughter of the king of the Sidonians, and a worshipper of Baal, the Canaanite false god of fertility.

Ahab was evil to begin with, but he was also greatly influenced by his wife. After her beloved prophets of Baal were humiliated and killed on Mt. Carmel, Jezebel went after Elijah with a vengeance! What made Jezebel so dangerous, besides her relentless pursuit of God's man, Elijah? It was her influence among God's people, encouraging them to compromise. She convinced her husband to pollute the worship of the One True God with the pagan worship of her homeland. Fiercely tenacious, she had many of Israel's true prophets who openly opposed her put to death.

The spirit of Jezebel is one that encourages compromise. In a city where the power of the trade unions was great, there were those in the church in Thyatira who were leading their fellow believers to compromise their allegiance to Christ by participating in the temple feasts. Just as Jezebel claimed to worship the God of Israel, so these compromisers claimed to follow Jesus. Jesus clearly described the consequences of the failure to repent as follows:

> I have given her time to repent of her immorality, but she is unwilling. So I will cast her on a bed of suffering, and I will make those who commit adultery with her suffer intensely, unless they repent of her ways. I will strike her children dead. Then all the churches will know that I am he who searches hearts, and minds, and I will repay each of you according to your deeds.
>
> (Revelation 2:21-23 NIV)

Just like Jezebel met a violent death (see 2 Kings 9:30-37), Jesus promised judgment to those who cause believers to compromise in Thyatira. It is hard to believe this was all happening in the church—or is it? Aren't there present-day parallels to this scenario? I'm not saying that trade unions are inherently evil, or that today we are surrounded by pagan temples where church members go to eat meat sacrificed to idols, but isn't the spirit of Jezebel alive and well in our world today? What accounts for all the compromise among many who make weekly pilgrimages to church buildings of all shapes, sizes, and denominations?

It seems to me, a lack of faith and trust in God is at the core. Talk is cheap, you know? Anyone who has spent any time in church at all can come up with a religious sounding prayer or sterilized statement of faith, but what about when the rubber meets the road? When push comes to shove, how many are willing to walk forward with nothing but the Word of God as assurance? What do you think would happen if more *would?* "And my God will meet all your needs according to the riches of his glory in Christ Jesus." (Philippians 4:19 NIV) "Look at the birds. They don't plant or harvest or store food in barns, for your heavenly Father feeds them. And aren't you far more valuable to him than they are?" (Matthew 6:26 NLT) "But seek ye first the kingdom of God, and his righteousness; and all these things shall be added unto you." (Matthew 6:33 KJV)

In his book, *Why Revival Tarries*, Leonard Ravenhill wrote: "Some day someone is going to pick up this book (the Bible) and believe it, and put us all to shame."[9] Lord, let it be me! Let it be the Church of today! What do you think would happen if the Church moved forward against Jezebel's temptation to compromise, walking in faith in the One who has a proven track record—Jesus, the same yesterday, today, forever! Should more energy be expended leading others away from Jezebel's compromise than lobbying Congress to pass laws that are only as good as the paper they're printed on? Seriously, since when has a law curbed the desires of the human heart? It didn't work for Israel, and it won't work for America. As always, Jesus gave a promise to those in Thyatira who would repent:

> *To the one who is victorious and does my will to the end, I will give authority over the nations—that one "will rule them with an iron scepter and will dash them to pieces like pottery"—just*

as I have received authority from my Father. I will also give that one the morning star. Whoever has ears, let them hear what the Spirit says to the churches.

(Revelation 2:26-29 NIV)

Thyatira was a small city with a small church, but in Christ, the smallest church can have the greatest influence! The promised reward to the faithful is positions of authority, demonstrating that perseverance is crucial to the Christian. This portion of the passage, "*will rule them with an iron scepter and will dash them to pieces like pottery,*" comes from Isaiah 30:14, speaking of the

consequences of disobedience to God. The claims of superior knowledge of the ones who were leading some astray will come to nothing. Their false beliefs will crumble. The ones who persevere and stay true to God will rule over those who now persecute them.

The *morning star* is a symbol for Christ, here contrasted to the sun god, Apollo, widely worshipped in Thyatira. While Apollo was viewed as the god of light, among other positive attributes, it is Jesus who is *real* light, *pure* light! The recurring phrase, *whoever has ears, let them hear,* not only makes the promise to all who are willing to listen, it also infers that not all will. Today, Jesus extends to us the same promise for those who refuse to compromise on matters of holiness of heart and life. Let us be among those who are victorious and do the Lord's will—to the end!

CHAPTER FOURTEEN

The Church at Sardis – Revelation 3:1-6

What's in a name? Proverbs 22:1 says, "A good name is more desirable than great riches; to be esteemed is better than silver or gold," but what if the name only goes skin deep; what if the reputation far exceeds the truth? In our advertising-driven society, what looks good on the outside may be rotten on the inside. The same is true with people. So many times, celebrated persons look glamourous and beautiful on film, yet their personal lives are disastrous!

This was the case with the church in Sardis, the one that had a reputation of being alive, but was spiritually dead. This church may have fooled a lot of people, but to Jesus, who "holds the seven spirits of God and the seven stars" (Revelation 3:1 NIV), the true condition is known. The city of Sardis was wealthy and prosperous; the church experienced little persecution; therefore, it was allowed to grow and thrive as the *"get along"* church. The church enjoyed a prominent status, perhaps even ranking high on the local social status as a good place to belong.

Apparently, though, there was still hope; there were still some hot coals glowing underneath the dead religion that had replaced its once raging fire. Jesus said there remained some people

who were still walking with Him, who had not gone the way of the majority. Sadly, that's as close to a commendation as Christ could offer this dying church. He offers hope, not for the church as a whole, but for the remnant whose names He would not remove from the Book of Life.

Many see the western Church reflected here. The Great American Church has sent many missionaries to all parts of the world, but is now a shell of her former self. The buildings and institutions founded with Christian zeal are now reduced to stone, brick, and plaster, and a page in a history book. Monuments to the memory of visionaries and leaders of mighty movements now only collect dust and cost way too much to maintain.

Thank God, though, for the remnant! Thank God for those who have not soiled their garments with the sin of complacency! Thank God for those who see the mighty hand of God in the present and the future—not just in the past! There is an ever-growing, powerful representation of the body of Christ emerging in our nation and in our world, while simultaneously, the dying, decaying Church of Sardis slips into the pages of history. The fires of genuine revival not only empower the waking, but they also consume the dead and dying. Thank God for those who are awakening in this hour; thank God for His patience and love extended toward those who have been rescued from a Sardis-like stupor!

What do you think ***will*** happen as those redeemed by the blood of the Lamb continue to stand up and be counted among the faithful? These who embrace renewed life and experience in Christ as a supernatural daily expectation are understanding their position and authority in Christ, relegating to the trash heap what remains of cultural Christianity. A couple of things are happening as a result; the church of Sardis is complaining about it, longing for the good old days, and the newly energized, holy Bride of Christ is walking forward in her white clothing, ready to meet her Bridegroom! As we come ever nearer to the return of Christ, let us strip off anything that may be slowing us down, including past accomplishments and reputation, and run the race to completion!

CHAPTER FIFTEEN

The Church at Philadelphia – Revelation 3:7-13

Philadelphia, located along the Roman Road to the east of Sardis, was nicknamed "Little Athens," because of its many pagan temples and festivities. Its geographical location made it the gateway to the east; it bordered Phrygia, Mysia, and Lydia. It was noted for its hot springs, its grapes (and its wine) and, according to early church leader Ignatius, a large population of hostile Jews. They presented a great danger to Christians, along with the pagan worship which was so prevalent. The city still exists, now known as Alaşehir, however, the people are predominantly Muslim. The glory of the church described by Jesus in John's letter is long gone.

Philadelphia, along with Smyrna, received no condemnation from Jesus. The enemies of the first-century church here came from the outside, not from within. Verse 8 sums up both the qualities of this small church and the heart of Jesus toward them. He said, "I know your deeds. See, I have placed before you an open door that no one can shut. I know that you have little strength, yet you have kept my word and have not denied my name."

The term *little strength* could mean numbers or influence, or both; what's important to know is that their faithfulness has come to the Lord's attention, and He will reward them for it! Verse 9 describes those of the *synagogue of Satan*. Jesus used this same terminology in His address to the Church in Smyrna. These are those who claim to be Jews but are liars, and Jesus promises to make them come under the authority of the Church in due time. Because this small church has been faithful, Jesus promises them *an open door that no one can shut.*

> Since you have kept my command to endure patiently, I will also keep you from the hour of trial that is going to come on the whole world to test the inhabitants of the earth.
>
> (Revelation 3:10 NIV)

This promise was given to other believers as well as those in Philadelphia. The Apostle Paul told the Christians in Thessalonica that Jesus would "save them from the coming wrath" (1 Thessalonians 1:10). We call this promise our *Blessed Hope*—the Rapture of the Church—not only in Philadelphia or Thessalonica, but for all believers who have the same spirit of obedience as the faithful few to whom our Lord made this promise almost 2,000 years ago. In Chapter 2:5, Jesus told the Ephesian church that He was coming, and if they didn't repent, He would "take away their lampstand." Here, He tells the Philadelphia Church that He's coming soon, but not as a warning, but as a promise of deliverance.

"I am coming soon. Hold on to what you have, so that no one will take your crown." (Revelation 3:11 NIV) This is something for us to ponder today. The church that is unknown to the world may be well-known to God! What the world elevates, God may not even notice; what is of great importance in the world's system may not be important to God. The admonition to us today is to do what is right and to do it often! What do you think would happen if the Church adopted the practices of the Philadelphians: to simply honor God even in trial and persecution? Are we guilty of responding in kind when godless people criticize us for our faith? What's the worst that could happen if we stopped doing that?

The American church is famous for drawing red, white, and blue lines of offense, and then daring others to cross them. So many feel their American citizenship gives them the right *not* to be offended. Here's a news flash: the Church has *always* been a target of offense by an unbelieving world! The One on whom rests the distinction of fulfilling the law and prophets was killed by unbelievers some of them very religious! What would Jesus say about the Church today, which spends more time in political action than in prayer? What do you think would happen if we truly trusted God—like the Philadelphians did—to settle accounts from a heavenly perspective and according to His timeline, and just be the Church that Jesus gave His life for?

> The one who is victorious I will make a pillar in the temple of my God. Never again will they leave it. I will write on them the name of my God and name of the city of my God, the New Jerusalem, which is coming down out of heaven from my God; and I will also write on them my new name. Whoever has ears, let him hear what the Spirit says to the churches.
>
> (Revelation 3:12-13 NIV)

CHAPTER SIXTEEN

The Church at Laodicea - Revelation 3:14-22

The problem of the Church in Laodicea was, they had no problems! None, at least, that they would admit to having. Along with the Church in Sardis, Laodicea received no commendation from Jesus, only condemnation. Laodicea was a wealthy city, known for its famous black wool and its collyrium, an eye salve that was known all over Asia Minor. The city was also a major banking center and was located at the intersection of two major trade routes, about fifty miles southeast of Philadelphia. The Church in Laodicea is referred to in Colossians 1:7, 4:12, and 4:16. From the context found there, it's assumed that the church was founded by Epaphras, a ministry partner of the Apostle Paul.

Laodicea was the *Lukewarm Church*. If Smyrna was *The Rich, Poor Church*, Laodicea was certainly *The Poor, Rich Church*. Its members couldn't handle success as the world measures it. They found themselves lacking nothing they couldn't buy! Prosperity had cooled the fire that once burned brightly in their midst. Jesus told them:

> I know your deeds, that you are neither cold nor hot. I wish you were either one or the other. So, because you are lukewarm—neither hot nor cold—I am about to spit you out of my mouth.
>
> (Revelation 3:15-16 NIV)

The analogy wouldn't have been lost on even a casual observer of geography in Asia Minor at the time this letter was written. Hierapolis to the north boasted of its hot springs, known for their healing properties. Colossae to the south was known for its refreshing cold waters streaming down from Mount Cadmus, used as both a supply of drinking water and for therapeutic purposes. In between these two cities lay Laodicea, with its prominent Church, neither cold nor hot—only lukewarm and good for nothing.

A lukewarm church is one professing Christianity without being affected by its fire! Its members claim to be self-sufficient in all ways, yet remain oblivious to their sinful condition. In keeping with its geographical location on the crossroads of commerce, the Laodicean Church was in the middle of the road. It was a church of no spiritual extremes. Jesus preferred they adopt a stance—be cold or be hot—so that He could make something of them! One who is spiritually cold can be made hot, but a lukewarm, lackadaisical attitude toward things holy acts as Novocain to the power of the Spirit. This was a major indictment for this church! There must not have been too many that could have been called "hot" for God, for Jesus makes no mention of a faithful remnant, but as is always the case, He offers the opportunity for repentance. "Those whom I love I rebuke and discipline. So be earnest and repent." (Revelation 3:19 NIV)

It's a bad place to be—in danger of judgment and knowing better! It's not difficult to see parallels to the twenty-first century Church in this short address to the Laodicean Christians of the late first century. For years, commentators have equated the American Church with the Church of Laodicea—ambivalent, lethargic, spiritually unaware, but thank God, we still live in the age of grace! Jesus warned this ancient Church by saying,

> You say, "I am rich; I have acquired wealth and do not need a thing." But you do not realize that you are wretched, pitiful, poor, blind, and naked. I counsel you to buy from me gold refined in the fire, so you can become rich; and white clothes to wear, so you can cover your shameful nakedness; and salve to put on your eyes, so you can see.
>
> (Revelation 3:17-18 NIV)

The Church in the city that boasted in its wealth and high standard of living had compromised its dependence upon God. The fine garments that were produced from its rare black wool and the notoriety that came from its renowned eye salve had caused believers there to be naked and blind in the eyes of Jesus. Jesus wanted them to experience true prosperity by embracing relationship with God over self-reliance and worldly acclaim. For the members of the Church in Laodicea, all the things they thought they were, they weren't. They had all the gold they wanted, but not the gold of heaven's refineries. They had all the clothes they wanted, but they lacked the clothes of Christ's righteousness. Their medical school was a world leader in eye salve, yet spiritually speaking, they couldn't see. Jesus invites them as He says, "Here I am! I stand at the door and knock. If anyone hears my voice and opens the door, I will come in and eat with that person, and they with me." (Revelation 3:20 NIV)

I remember a painting located front and center on the front wall of the church I grew up in; you may have had the same painting in your church. It's a depiction of Jesus knocking on a door with the words, "Behold, I stand at the door and knock." Through the ages, we have used this painting and this scripture to show the heart of Christ; that He loves us so much that He never ceases to invite us to follow Him. Many have noticed the fact that the door upon which Jesus knocks has no doorknob on the outside; each person must willingly open the door to receive Him. While this is a beautiful picture of the heart of Jesus, the scripture more accurately addresses the Church, specifically, the Church in Laodicea. If we are to draw an accurate parallel, we must admit that it's the door of the *Church* that Jesus is knocking on; it is to the already found that Jesus makes His impassioned plea, "Won't you let Me in so we can get back to what's important?"

The lukewarm church is busy about nothing. The lukewarm church acts just like the world but claims a distinction based upon the memory of something that no longer exists. Living in a lukewarm condition is accepting you have just enough religion to keep you out of hell, but not enough to be dangerous to the enemy of your soul. Not hot and not cold, lukewarmness sits on the fence of complacency with little sense of urgency about spiritual things. Genuine moves of God are reduced to stories of a time gone by before self-sufficiency, glory, and prosperity replaced the fire of the Holy Spirit.

What do you think would happen if *First Memorial Church* moved all its memorial plaques out of the front lobby and into the basement where they belong, focusing instead on what is *yet* to come? What do you think would change if the lukewarm church repented and got hot again for Jesus? We don't have to wonder; Jesus promised the Laodicean Church and He promises us today, "To the one who is victorious, I will give the right to sit with me on my throne, just as I was victorious and sat down with my Father on his throne." (Revelation 3:21 NIV)

CONCLUSION

According to Revelation 1:4, this letter is addressed "to the seven churches in the province of Asia." Because of this, I'm convinced all the churches had something to learn from the sections to their sister congregations. The same is true today, isn't it? Can't we all gain insight into God's holy plan for all who call Jesus Lord? There isn't room for shaming or thinking ourselves better-than when considering the enormity of the task Jesus left us with after He ascended. Jesus is coming for a spotless Church—a holy, faultless Church. The Apostle Paul framed this so well in Ephesians chapter 5, where he likens a husband's obligations to his wife to the attitude that Christ has toward His Church.

> For husbands, this means love your wives, just as Christ loved the church. He gave up his life for her to make her holy and clean, washed by the cleansing of God's word. He did this to present her to himself as a glorious church without a spot or wrinkle or any other blemish. Instead, she will be holy and without fault.
>
> (Ephesians 5:25-27 NLT)

Jesus offers a common admonishment to all seven of these congregations when He says, "Whoever has ears, let them hear what the Spirit says to the churches." (Revelation 2:7a; 2:11a; 2:17a; 2:29; 3:6; 3:13; 3:22) We have a sacred obligation to allow the Lord to continue to change us so that we never find ourselves unprepared. It's important to remember, as a safeguard against apostacy, that each of the seven churches of Revelation had an earnest beginning! To think oneself incapable of falling away is a dangerous attitude to have. Having spiritual ears tuned to the

Holy Spirit is the only way to stay on track, unspoiled by the world we call our temporary home.

In our fast-paced and rapidly changing world, we do well to understand that not much, foundationally, has really changed at all since the close of the New Testament. For example, the account of the Seven Churches of Asia, which we looked at in the second part of this book, has not changed. Mankind has been attempting to rationalize sin ever since the fall in the garden of Eden. Centuries before the current identity crisis fad that has many of us shaking our heads in disbelief, millions of people have self-identified as *Christian* without any evidence of the transforming work of the Holy Spirit in their lives. Before new age and mysticism became mainstream, quite a few churchgoers were already comfortably settled in pluralistic mindsets, mixing traditions of men with scripture. As a result, there have developed strongly held religious beliefs that have no source in God's Word, but are cherished as if they did. If you don't believe me, try challenging them!

Lots of Questions

Because of this, I wonder if it's actually *awakening* rather than *revival* that we need. For something to be "revived," it must have existed in the first place. You can't revive something that never lived! Is it possible that so many of our churches are powerless because their members have never been born again? Do we try to define what a Christian is by other than Biblical standards? Have we made it too easy to be labeled *Christian*? Have denominational labels served only to make us feel better about remaining in our sin and disobedience because we can always blame the problems of the church on *those people*? Have denominations run their course? What does God really think about all our songs, books, church services, and religious programming? Which type of church is closest to the New Testament model? If one claims this distinction, haven't they automatically forfeited their bragging rights since they have theoretically become a cult by dismissing everyone else?

I've got to be honest—these types of questions run through my mind regularly. The older I get, the more amazed I am at the patience of God. Even with all her warts, the true Church will one day present herself to her Groom as a spotless bride, without spot or wrinkle! Incredible! Jesus loves His Church so much that He has promised to forever make her victorious over the gates of hell, all the while never leaving or forsaking her. Can we stop for just a moment and shout, *Hallelujah*?! After almost 40 years in public ministry, after thousands of miles, songs, and sermons, and after many disappointments and heartaches, I still love the Church of Jesus Christ! There is no finer institution on earth for redeeming the lost, nurturing the found, feeding the hungry, and healing the sick. Without the Church, we would have fewer hospitals, schools, and universities. We would be poorer in the arts: music, painting, drama, and poetry. The rapidly deteriorating morals in our society would be gone entirely without the positive influence of the Church evident in our history and culture.

Yes, the Church is worth fighting for. In admitting that, we must turn inward, recognizing that we are the Church! When we criticize the Church, we have to take a long, hard look inward, as we have the power to either improve or degrade her by our attitude. If you are born again, if you have been transformed by the Holy Spirit and are continuing to be transformed, *you are the Church*! What do you think would happen if you set out to be a reformer, a revivalist, a positive influence? What do you think would happen if you walked forward, from this moment on, dedicated to living like Jesus, for Jesus, because of Jesus, no matter what might come your way? Don't you think the Church, the world, and the kingdom of God would be respectively healed, blessed, and expanded? Could it really be that simple?

If you have never allowed God to have His way in your life, I pray you'll do it today. I'm not going to give you a sinner's prayer to pray or a suggestion of a particular church to join, but know this; if you have come to the end of yourself and are ready to follow Jesus, the Holy Spirit will change you and make you new. Jesus, as God in the flesh, already did the work for you. He lived a sinless life, yet paid sin's price with His own blood for everyone who will believe on Him as Savior and Lord. Christ then defeated death by rising from the grave and ascending into heaven. He lives today, making intercession for us before His Father in heaven. God and the Son send the Holy Spirit to indwell every believer; as a believer, you'll never again be alone! Your prayer of faith today will be the start of a new life in Christ—the beginning of eternity, each day becoming transformed more into the image of Jesus! Get connected with a local church that believes the Bible. Make this church better by your prayers, your presence, by giving of yourself, your time, talents, gifts, and finances! Get into God's Word so it will get into you! Celebrate Jesus every day! Embrace all that God has for you! Live out the person God created you to be! Be the Church! What do *you* think *will* happen…when?

NOTES

1 Recalled as a personal dictum in *Letter from the Archbishop of the West Indies* in Theology (1956), vol. 59. This quote has also been referenced in many other works.

2 Cymbala, Jim; Merrill, Dean, Fresh Power: *What Happens When God Leads and You Follow* (Zondervan, 2003)

3 Bounds, E.M., *Power Through Prayer* (Trinity Press; Unabridged edition, December 9, 2011)

4 Barna, George, *New Insights into the Generation of Growing Influence: Millennials in America* (Foundations of Freedom, October, 2021)

5 https://get.tithe.ly/blog/what-is-generosity-answers-differ-for-each-generation-according-to-barna-report

6 *God's Generals: Why They Succeeded and Why Some Fail* (Volume 1): Liardon, Roberts: 8582086411113: Amazon.com: Books. These books are also available through other booksellers. In addition, you can access many videos pertaining to these books online.

7 https://gracequotes.org/author-quote/leonard-ravenhill/

8 www.dinnerchurch.com is a good place to get more information about this movement.

9 Ravenhill, Leonard, *Why Revival Tarries* (Bethany Press, 1959)

Printed in the USA
CPSIA information can be obtained
at www.ICGtesting.com
CBHW070345240324
5747CB00009B/58

9 798893 330984